Bearing Witness to Epiphany

SUNY series in Contemporary Continental Philosophy

Dennis J. Schmidt, editor

Bearing Witness to Epiphany

Persons, Things, and the Nature of Erotic Life

John Russon

Published by State University of New York Press, Albany

For information, contact State University of New York Press, Albany, NY
www.sunypress.edu

Production by Diane Ganeles
Marketing by Anne M. Valentine

Library of Congress Cataloging-in-Publication Data

Russon, John Edward, 1960–
   Bearing witness to epiphany : persons, things, and the nature of erotic life /
John Russon.
       p. cm. — (SUNY series in contemporary continental philosophy)
   Includes bibliographical references and index.
   ISBN 978-1-4384-2503-0 (hardcover : alk. paper) — ISBN 978-1-4384-2504-7
(pbk. : alk. paper) 1. Philosophical anthropology. 2. Life. I. Title.
   BD450.R788 2009
   128—dc22

                                                                    2008020824

                              10 9 8 7 6 5 4 3 2 1

This work is dedicated to Kirsten Elisabeth Jacobson,
whose constant companionship and partnership
in philosophical exploration made this writing possible.

But it is natural that such friendships should be infrequent, for
such people are rare.

—Aristotle, *Nicomachean Ethics*

The reality of the world in which the children eventually must live as adults is one in which every loyalty involves something of an opposite nature which might be called a disloyalty, and the child who has had the chance to reach to all these things in the course of growth is in the best position to take a place in such a world. Eventually, if one goes back, one can see that these disloyalties, as I am calling them, are an essential feature of living, and they stem from the fact that it is disloyal to everything that is not oneself if one is to be oneself. The most aggressive and therefore the most dangerous words in the languages of the world are to be found in the assertion *I AM*. It has to be admitted, however, that only those who have reached a stage at which they can make this assertion are really qualified as adult members of society.

—D. W. Winnicott, "The Child in the Family Group," in *Home Is Where We Start From*

Learn, in life, art; in the artwork, learn life.
If you see the one right, you see the other also.

—Friedrich Hölderlin, "To Himself," from *Odes and Epigrams*

CONTENTS

♦♦♦

ACKNOWLEDGMENTS

♦♦♦

As I read through the many pages of this manuscript, checking the final version for the last time, I am struck repeatedly by the dependence of so many of the specific thoughts on my interactions with particular people—my friends, my colleagues, and my students. Len Lawlor, Ed Casey, John Sallis, Réal Fillion, Doug Anderson, and Graeme Nicholson are professional colleagues and friends whose thoughtful philosophical work has been importantly formative for my thinking about matters in this book. Catherine Zuckert, Michael Zuckert, and Nicholas Capaldi gave me the opportunities to participate with them in seminars hosted by the Liberty Fund, and my conversations with them laid the foundations for a number of the thoughts in this book. I have had the good fortune as well to be able to work closely with a large number of highly insightful and highly articulate musicians and visual artists, who also have contributed greatly to my thinking, most notably Luis Jacob, Ken Aldcroft, Justin Haynes, Wayne Cass, Mike Milligan, Peter Hill, Ron Davis, Nick Fraser, Arthur Goldstein, Chris Gale, Chris Banks, and Victor Bateman. I owe the greatest debt to my close friends and students, interactions with whom have been my primary site for learning: Maria Talero, Patricia Fagan, Kirsten Jacobson, Peter Simpson, Kym Maclaren, David Ciavatta, David Morris, Peter Costello, Bruce Gilbert, Cory Styranko, Jessica Brotman, Brian Mackintosh, Eve Rabinoff, Whitney Howell, Tristana Martin Rubio, Don Beith, Andrea Sentesy, Scott Marratto, Shannon Hoff, Susan Bredlau, Kai Matthews, Eric Sanday, Greg Recco, and Greg Kirk. I thank as well the many university teachers who have used my book *Human Experience* in their classrooms and the wonderful students I have met when I have been invited to visit those classes: the many sorts of feedback I have received through those encounters—and the friends I have made—have been a great resource in the writing of this book.

INTRODUCTION

♦♦♦

This book is fundamentally about what it is, and what it is like, to be a person. Each of us is a person, and my attempt in this book is to describe the world in the terms in which that world exists for a person, that is, to describe the world in the terms in which it actually matters for each of us. All of our sciences study the world in some way, but the terms of these sciences are not the terms of our living experience: the particles of the physicist exist in a context of the complex technology of modern instruments of measurement coupled with highly complex theories, but they are not functioning elements of anyone's living experience; the statistical analyses of the sociologist may be helpful in accurately predicting patterns of social behavior, but no one lives as "an average white American teenager." Whatever value these sciences offer—and no doubt they offer great value— none of them is, or purports to be, an analysis of the world *as it is lived by us*, none of them is a description of the inherently *human* world. This book is an attempt to be just that: it is an attempt to describe reality *as we live it*, an attempt to establish the terms in which a human life is meaningful.

What makes a life meaningful? We find meaning in our lives through our aspirations and accomplishments, through the others we admire and care for, through our myriad daily practices, and through our hobbies, careers, and entertainments, our religious practices, and so on. It is these, the matters of everyday life, with which we shall be concerned here. Our study will be about aspirations, occupations, and most especially our relationships with other people. It is in these domains that we shall find the matters of deepest significance in the life of the person. The ultimate focus of this book will be on our dealings with other people in the context of developing a meaningful life, but to get there we will first engage in a substantial discussion of the nature of *things*.

It is primarily in and through things that we live. Our world is populated with things. We often explicitly notice the many individual objects

1

around us, such as the package left at the neighbor's doorstep, the cat that comes up to greet me, or the new jacket you are wearing, but even when we do not explicitly notice them, as, for example, when I open a door or wipe my boots on a mat while being absorbed in a conversation, all of our ongoing activities are conducted through interaction with things. These "worldly" and public things are typically things that I experience as "not me" and "not mine." We also deal with things in an importantly different way, however. We typically depend on defining ourselves through those things that we call our own, whether our dwelling places, our clothes, or our favorite personal possessions. We also depend on a special relationship we have to those things that we make, and through which we express ourselves. In these latter cases, we do not experience things as "not me" or "not mine" but, quite the contrary, it is in and through them that we have our very experience of "me" and "mine." Our study of what it is to be a person and of what the terms of meaningfulness are in a human life will especially take us into this domain of things that we "enown": as we consider what it is to be one's "own" self, we will especially be led to consider questions of our ownership of things, and also to consider our involvement with things as media for creative self-expression. We will see that things are not primarily meaningful in our world as detached, impersonal objects but that, most importantly, it is through an engagement with and immersion of our own identity in things that the aspirations, occupations, and relationships that are most important to us are established.

It is through our study of things that we shall be able to pose the question: "What is a person?" and, more specifically, "What is another person?" We shall see that the other person is a unique kind of reality that offers to us the possibility for creative growth and development beyond the limited horizons that we are able to supply to ourselves. In studying the role of others in the formation of personal identity, we shall first consider the distinctive role of the family. Here we shall consider the crucially formative role those particular individuals who make up the family play in initiating the individual person into the experience of shared human life. We shall then contrast the distinctive character of family experience with the form of experience that will be our central concern in the remainder of the book: erotic relationships. Unlike family experiences, in which one has one's others "given" to one, and in which one is defined as a "member," erotic relationships are freely adopted, and one functions in them as a free individual. Through discussing these dimensions of our experience, we shall see that, contrary to many familiar descriptions that denigrate sexuality, erotic life is in fact the dynamic center of the meaningfulness of developed human life; erotic life is the real sphere of human *freedom*, that is, of creativity and responsibility. It is the ultimate "point" of our study to develop from this description of the erotic domain an understanding of ethics, that is, an understanding of how and why matters of justice and responsibility are essential to the life of a person. What we shall see, in short, is that human reality is *essentially* shared, that this shared reality is rooted in creativity, and that this shared space of creativity inherently brings with it norms of care, justice, honesty, and openness. We shall find that in the human world ethics and reality are in a kind of reciprocity, reality inherently calling us to ethical responsibility, and ethics fundamentally calling us to grasp reality as a norm.

In developing this line of thought, this book, *Bearing Witness to Epiphany*, stands as a companion to my earlier book, *Human Experience: Philosophy, Neurosis, and the Elements of Everyday Life*. In that earlier work I used the insights of contemporary European philosophy to develop an interpretation and analysis of the nature of mental health. That work studied in more detail than this one the child's experience of family life and the impact this has on the (healthy or unhealthy) form of our adult engagement with the world. This work complements and extends the argument of *Human Experience*, especially through its focus on sexuality, and the emergence of the experience of individuality in adolescent life. Also, whereas *Human Experience* revolved more or less around what I would call an "epistemological" orientation, in that it asked after the processes and practices by which we come to form our meaningful experience ("knowledge") of the world, this work revolves more around the axis of metaphysics, attempting to characterize accurately the nature of reality and moving from there into matters of ethics, attempting to characterize accurately the nature of values as those emerge within our experience. These themes of epistemology, metaphysics, and ethics—and, to be sure, the central themes of the development of personal identity and of meaningfulness in human life—are among the oldest, deepest, and most difficult (and, indeed, most important) matters of philosophical investigation. My goal in this book, though, like my goal in *Human Experience*, is to present these matters in a way that is accessible to a nonspecialist reader and that, without sacrificing rigor, presents these matters in a way that is clear and that clearly demonstrates their relevance to the most pressing matters of everyday life.

Though this book, like *Human Experience*, is an original work of philosophy, it again draws heavily on the insights of many great philosophers both of our contemporary world and of our distant past. Most manifestly, this is a work of philosophy within the tradition of continental European philosophy as that developed in the nineteenth and twentieth centuries. The central ideas in this work about the nature of persons, of artistic creation, of things, and of justice are highly dependent on the insights especially of

German philosophers Martin Heidegger, G. W. F. Hegel, and Friedrich Schiller, and of French philosophers Maurice Merleau-Ponty, Jean-Paul Sartre, and Jacques Derrida. Though this book will not directly address any of these thinkers, it is nonetheless my hope that it will, like *Human Experience*, also serve as a useful text for introducing students or other interested readers to some of the central themes and concepts of these great thinkers. Though I shall not be discussing these philosophers directly in the upcoming chapters, I can offer a few words of orientation to the interested reader regarding how I understand my work to be related to the works of other thinkers in our philosophical tradition.

I have said that this work operates within the arena of contemporary continental philosophy, and this is quite true; even more deeply, though, this work is indebted to the philosophical insights of the great philosophers of ancient Greece, Plato and Aristotle. It is Aristotle who brilliantly articulated the insight that "all men by nature desire to know" (*Metaphysics* A.1). In this remark, Aristotle identifies the nature of things and the nature of humanity to be inherently and intimately united, and it will be the articulation of this insight that will ultimately be the central idea of this book. Aristotle's notion of *phusis*—that is, reality as self-emergent—and his notion of the human as the animal with *logos* (the ability to "take account") are also ideas very much at the foundation of the work in this book. Indeed, there is good reason to construe each of Hegel, Heidegger, and Merleau-Ponty as themselves fundamentally carrying on and developing creatively this same Aristotelian tradition in philosophy, and, in part, my own conjoining of Aristotelian insights with the ideas of later European thinkers is an attempt to highlight an inherent continuity between Aristotelian and contemporary European philosophy. Further, in his great philosophical insights, Aristotle is himself, to my mind, carrying on some of the deepest threads of the Platonic philosophy and, ultimately, it is this Platonic philosophy with which I understand myself to be engaged. This book can be understood as my attempt to grapple with the insights of Plato's *Apology, Crito, Symposium,* and *Ion* in particular, and to think along with them in trying to apprehend better the nature of the human being in relation to other people, to justice, to art, and to reality in general. In particular, I draw from the *Apology* and *Crito* the notion that a commitment to justice is the attitude in which human nature matures, and I draw from the *Symposium* and *Ion* the notion that it is in the domains of erotic attraction and artistic creation that human growth is primarily accomplished.

My development of all the themes of human nature, justice, and sexuality draws heavily upon the insights into the interpersonal dimensions of personal life found in Heidegger's discussion of "being-with" in *Being and Time*, in Hegel's discussion of the dialectic of recognition in his *Phenomenology of Spirit*, in Sartre's discussion of "Concrete Relations with

Others" in *Being and Nothingness*, and in Merleau-Ponty's discussions of sexuality and language in his *Phenomenology of Perception*. My discussion of the *thing* has been powerfully shaped by the work of Heidegger, who studies the thing as object, equipment, and artwork, and my central focus on the foundational role of artistic expression in human development has strong resonance with the ideas in his "Origin of the Work of Art," as well as those in Friedrich Schiller's *Letters on the Aesthetic Education of Man*. My discussion of art and language also is significantly influenced by Jacques Derrida's many writings on the nature of language, especially the theme of "iterability," found, for example, in his essay "Signature, Event, Context." My discussion of the thing as property has been most powerfully shaped by the work of Hegel and also by the work of twentieth-century psychologists; indeed, students of continental philosophy in general would be wise to pay greater attention to the work of figures such as D. W. Winnicott, Salvador Minuchin, and R. D. Laing, among others. My discussion of the nature of our own body and its relation to these different aspects of the thing has been most powerfully shaped by the work of Merleau-Ponty. My writing is also strongly influenced by a number of other writers, the most important of whom for this work are John Locke, Immanuel Kant, Karl Marx, Ralph Waldo Emerson, Sigmund Freud, R. G. Collingwood, John Dewey, Gilles Deleuze, and Félix Guattari. Though I almost never make specific reference to their works, the role of their insights will be manifest to the attuned reader on every page.

The book itself is organized to take the reader from something like "first principles," that is, the general terms in which all experience in general is to be understood, to the intricacies of the specific, developed forms of experience that make human life meaningful: we shall move in our argument from a discussion of the most basic form of sense to a discussion of the fullest development of freedom. The first chapter of the book is roughly methodological, the second is loosely metaphysics, the third epistemology, and the fourth ethics. Each of these fields, in its articulation, invokes the others, with the result that ultimately no strict delimitation of these spheres is possible. This inseparability of the domains of metaphysics, epistemology, and ethics also means, as the fifth chapter will conclude, that being, by its nature, is to be known, and its reality is rooted in the ought, that knowledge must recognize its role in the constitution of reality, and that ethics must recognize that our duty is fulfilled in philosophy.

More specifically, chapter 1, "Initiations," argues that a notion of form is essential to a theory of human experience, that form is always experienced as an emergent or epiphanic reality, and that such epiphanies of form must be realized bodily. This chapter especially investigates our experience of music as exemplary for revealing the different dimensions of our experience of meaningful form. Chapter 2, "Ambiguity," develops a metaphysics of embodiment that is oriented by the need to explain the phenomenon of the epiphany of form. The body is shown to be an ambiguous structure that is always simultaneously itself and a propulsion beyond itself. This dynamic ambiguity of the body will serve as a paradigm for understanding the nature of things in general. Chapter 3, "Learning and Insight," develops a theory of knowledge that is consistent with the metaphysics of bodily ambiguity. In particular, it focuses on the need to explain the phenomenon of learning, that is, the process by which we transform our relationship to things from one of alienation to one of integration, and the phenomenon of insight that is the culmination of this process. We will see that learning about the nature of the world and learning about the nature of oneself are paired experiences and, further, that this learning takes place in an essentially intersubjective context. We will here note the distinctive and essential educative role played by our family experience (the topic that *Human Experience* investigated in detail) and also the essential role of artistic expression in our education and development. Chapter 4, "Responsibility," shows that the concept of the "person" is essential to understanding the kind of being that is a body and that can have insight and participate in the learning discussed in chapter 3. It studies the way that experiencing oneself as a person is something accomplished most fundamentally in the context of erotic relations with other persons. This chapter's central study of the nature of erotic life reveals that the natural development of our sexuality impels us to experiences of self-transformation that implicate us in experiences of responsibility regarding ourselves and other persons. We will see why it is essential to our development that we realize our individuality through the possession of property, but also why this experience of ownership naturally implicates us in relations of social responsibility and, ultimately, a politics of multiculturalism. Chapter 5, "Art and Philosophy," concludes the book by showing that the issues of self-transformation and responsibility explored in chapter 4 only exist and can only be dealt with in the sphere of human life that is made possible through communication, which rests upon our expressive, that is, artistic, capacities. Thus our expressive life is at the heart of our human experience, and the chapter explores the developmental, systematic way in which this is so. Philosophy, finally, is understood as the attempt to live up to the responsibilities of the human sphere, specifically understood as a creative sphere.

In this book I am looking for the *roots*, the dynamic sources, of our reality. I am looking for what the Greeks would call the *archai*. This is a book about growth, about the dynamic, self-transforming character of our life, the life that develops from these roots. It is a book about affirming the *reality* of the things we care about, and it is an antireductionist book, that is, it is an argument against those sorts of philosophy that try to explain away the everyday terms in which we experience our own world. The topics of study, especially in the later chapters, will be familiar issues of normal life. My philosophical project is to find the proper context for understanding them: precisely finding their roots. In my view, most of our problems come from a failure to understand the roots of what we experience. I will not try to solve all of our problems, but in trying to determine the roots of our experience I am trying to contribute to this project.

Kant argued that there is a priori scaffolding of experience, such that the meaning of our experience is always structured in terms of cause and effect, substance and accident, reality, negation, universality, and so on. Heidegger identified the form of our experience as projection, attunement, discourse, being-with, being-alongside, and so on. In what follows, I do not consider myself to be challenging these insights of Kant and Heidegger but to be thinking with them to a point of greater determinacy. Under the designation "the bodily a priori" or the designation "inexhaustibles," I will find such things as rhythm, things, understanding, family, law, property, dignity, learning, insight, tragedy, gods, marriage, betrayal, truth, responsibility, dance, marks, persons, humanity, and more. This is another way of saying that I will be arguing that the terms of our everyday experience are not optional. Let us turn now to the study of these elements of everyday life.

Part 1

The Epiphany
of the Real

1

♦♦♦

Initiations

On Method

M usic is not exclusively of the ear, or of the mind. It is of the body as a whole. Though it may require the involvement of ear and mind, music is not fully appreciated when it is severed from an engagement with the moving body. To receive music as music is to dance. The ear is certainly relevant to the experience of music—indeed, it is the necessary precondition for musical apprehension—but not the ear by itself, and not the ear of a contemplative intellect. The ear *of a body* is what is necessary to apprehend music, the ear as a magical portal by which an entirely new kind of reality can come to be within the world of my body. Music calls the body: it stirs the body to move, and it is only in the body's acceptance of this its transfigured status that the music is allowed to be.

The music is a phenomenon. It makes an appearance. In order to know what the nature of the music is, one must attend to the music itself: in advance of hearing, one does not know what the music is, but one must learn from the music what its specific character is. The music shows itself—it is an epiphany. Further, it shows itself as something compelling, something that dictates to the body how to behave. When the body dances, its limbs are moved by a power not its own. The music itself is the guide. The music is a reality: it is a causal force at play in the world. It informs the body. But this epiphany rests upon the properly supportive anticipative openness of the body. The music is real, but it cannot exist without the body's acts of preparation and realization. The music depends upon the body to allow it (the music) to be the causal force. Only within the anticipative openness of the body can the music realize its causal primacy, its authority.

11

The body is attuned to rhythm and music. The body finds itself open and attuned to the epiphany of such compelling forms, such compelling meanings. Such forms show themselves. These irreducible, given attunements cannot be proved through logic, nor can they be derived. They are revealed in and as "the a priori of the body," revealed incontrovertibly through the body's living experience. They are there for us to recognize and to describe, but whether or not they are there is not up to us, nor is an ultimate knowledge of why they are there within our power. We must be initiated into them, by them. These are the sorts of meanings that are available to us within the sort of world that is available to the sorts of bodies that we are. It is within the realms of significance opened up to us through these rhythms that our lives are elaborated.

As we proceed through this book we will be investigating these rhythms, these a priori attunements, that show themselves in our bodily lives. Our study of these "Urphenomena," as Goethe called them, these originary epiphanies of compelling form, will be neither exhaustive nor fully systematic. It will be, rather, a selective route through these fields, focusing specifically on matters that pertain to personal identity, self-expression, and sharing. Throughout, our primary concern will be to be honest in the description of these dimensions of our reality, and especially not to be reductive of the dimensions of openness, ambiguity and creativity that characterize our experience.

Rhythm

The three images in Figures 1.1–1.3 move from more simple to more complex. Each is a kind of "rhythm." First there is a simple repetition of pairs of dots. Second, a repeated geometrical pattern, with a beginning and an end. In these two images, it is relatively easy to see why I call these "rhythms": what we perceive in each case is a kind of regular sequence. The final image presents much more heterogeneous contours; it is the image of a face. I still refer to it as a kind of rhythm, though, inasmuch as a single meaning or style resonates throughout the whole of the image. Let us consider this further.

The images move from more simple to more complex, but what is noteworthy in each is that our perception of the image is not atomized, is not a composite of multiple, unrelated seeings. Rather, in each case we immediately see a meaningful form, a pattern of some sort that characterizes the image *as a whole. Within the perception* one aspect is linked to another rather than being held off simply in its own world. The first image is specially striking for this reason. It is virtually impossible for the viewer not to see the dots as grouped into pairs, with the close dots having a kind of "bond" between them. With effort, one can shift the emphasis and see the bond between the distant dots. (See Figures 1.4 and 1.5).

Figure 1.1

Figure 1.2

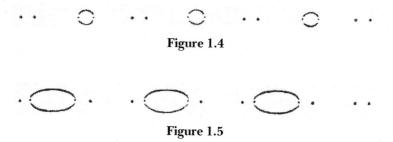

Figure 1.3

In either case, though, there is a form, a rhythm, perceived within the dots, a rhythm from which they cannot easily be perceptually isolated.

Something similar to this coupling of dots happens when we listen to music. To Western ears, a dominant seventh chord (for example, E7, produced by playing the notes E, G#, B, and D in unison) seems naturally to call for its resolution in a tonic chord (in this case, A major, produced by sounding the notes A, C#, and E in unison). The dominant seventh chord is not heard on its own in isolation from other sounds but, rather, assumes its sense only by invoking a larger context of sounds within which it points to its "home," its natural resolution in the tonic. Like the two dots in Figures 1.4 and 1.5, the two chords are heard *as*

Figure 1.4

Figure 1.5

"paired" (to use the language of Edmund Husserl), that is, the basic "unit" of our hearing is not the individual chord but the relationship of the chords, the chords in relation to each other: it is the structure of tension and resolution between the chords that is what is primarily heard. The *relationship* of resolution is the primary musical unit with which Western and other musical traditions work: it is the primary material, so to speak, out of which a musical composition is "made."

The latter two visual examples—the geometrical pattern and the image of the face—can be seen to be forms, or rhythms, in a sense analogous to that of the unity by resolution in music. We see the regular sequentiality of the geometrical pattern only because we see each part in light of the other parts: we see the second segment *as a repetition of* the first, and we see it in turn as leading to the third. Each segment stands to the others in relations of expectation and resolution, and the sense of the whole is how each segment responds to or resonates with the others. In the image of the face, too, we can see a similar structure of anticipation and fulfillment at work. We see some lines as making a nose manifest, but this is possible only because we see those lines in relation to the lines that make eyes manifest, and similarly in relation to the lines that mark cheeks, neck, ears, hair, and so on. Taken separately, any of the lines that make up the drawing of the face would "mean" nothing—they would simply be "squiggles," simply examples of different sorts of curves or line segments. Taken together, however, the sense of each resonates with the sense of all the others, answers to the expectations the others set, and through each the "rhythm" of the face is communicated. *For the vision that takes them together*, they are the compelling presentation of a form.

At the basic level, then, these are all examples of ways in which particular aspects of sense call for a resolution or response—a fulfillment—in another aspect of sense. The body's grasp of one such aspect of sense sets up in that body a felt need for—a propulsion toward—the other. The dots impel me to notice their regular pairing, and the music propels me to dance. In other settings, a doorknob calls to me to grasp and turn it, an open highway urges me to drive quickly, and the smooth, repetitive undulations of sand dunes invite me to wander aimlessly. It is this way that the body senses *as* a propulsion to fulfillment in further sense that I will call "rhythm." What we can see here is that sense and action are not separable: perception is a kind of acting, a bodily answering to a call that allows something to be realized.

In each case, what is revealed in rhythm is *form*, that is, a guiding meaningfulness that works *through* the manifold of sense without being reducible to the sum of the isolated occurrences of sense. Put otherwise, sense always *makes sense*, always has a direction, a meaning, a significance (even if that significance is confusion, contradiction, opacity, or incoherence). It is this significance that appears. Meaning is *revealed to us* in our sensing. This is the amazing character of ourselves—of our bodies: we are open to having significance revealed to us. We can be shown the forms of meaning.

These sensed bodily propulsions—these rhythms—are the original and originative meanings, the appearings of reality within the context of which our world of living experience is elaborated. Our experience begins as these rhythms, these bodily propulsions, these patterns of flow and interruption, of stop and start, of concentration and discharge, of desire and fulfillment, of question and answer, of resonance and interconnection, of integration and systematization, of disintegration and dissolution. The "units" or basic elements of experience are not disconnected atoms, but are little dramas that weave themselves together with and pull themselves away from others. It is within the element of meaning opened up by these original epiphanies that further, more developed meanings, more developed dramas, can emerge.

That this attitude of giving oneself over to the guiding force of rhythmic epiphany is more basic than the attitude of the self-conscious, goal-directed manipulation of limbs and world is important to understanding various situations of impaired human functioning. We typically think of ourselves as self-possessed intellects, as people who set explicit goals for ourselves that we then accomplish in the world through executing plans through utilizing our bodies upon the world. On this familiar "intellectual" model of the person, we understand ourselves as self-defined agents for whom the body is a vehicle and the world an alien object. Our model of our "musical" subjectivity, however, has shown us that our experience is rooted in an essential passivity, a magical responsiveness to compelling form that is more fundamental than the utilitarian approach to body and world. This priority of our musicality to our agency is suggested by the cases of Greg F. and Stephen Wiltshire, described by Oliver Sacks in *An Anthropologist on Mars*, for example, for whom the playing of music seems to offer access to the world of smooth body-world interaction that is otherwise denied them by a brain tumor and autism, respectively. Sacks acknowledges this deep-rooted musicality of our perception in his short essay "When Music Heals."

> For reasons we do not yet understand, musical abilities often are among the last to be lost, even in cases of widespread brain damage. . . . Some of my patients with strokes or Alzheimer's are unable to carry out a complex chain of actions: to dress, for example. Here, music can work as a mnemonic, a series of promptings in the form of verse or song, as in the childhood rhyme, "One, two, buckle my shoe." My patient Dr. P. had lost

the ability to recognize or identify even common objects, though he could see perfectly well. He was unable to recognize a glove or a flower when I handed it to him, and he once mistook his own wife for a hat. This condition was almost totally disabling, but he discovered that he could perform the needs and tasks of the day if they were organized in song. And so he had songs for dressing, songs for eating, songs for bathing, songs for everything. (4)

Music—rhythmic perception—is not a specialized case of a more basic nonmusical perception, as we typically presume when we assume that we are information-gathering machines, and that music is simply an entertaining use to which we put this normal perception. On the contrary, this "prosaic" stance of information gathering is in fact a derivate attitude that rests on a more basic musicality. It is only on the basis and in the context of an already musical relationship with the world that something like "detached observation" or "information gathering" becomes possible.

The Music of Everyday Life

I began with the phenomenon of music, and I led from this into rhythm. But in addition to what we normally call rhythm, music is also harmony and melody. We can develop our line of analysis further by integrating these other two notions—melody and harmony—with the first—rhythm. Let us begin with an approximate characterization of the basic senses of rhythm, harmony, and melody. Most simply, rhythm suggests the diachronic resounding of one moment of sense with another, that is, the way that the earlier sound anticipates and is fulfilled by a later sound: repetition. Harmony most basically suggests the synchronic resounding through different aspects of sense, that is, the way in which different notes that are currently sounding anticipate and fulfill each other: simultaneity. Melody fundamentally suggests the orientation and nonuniformity that characterize such resounding, that is, the experience that the sense leads from . . . to . . . : development. Let us go beyond this initial, approximate characterization and look a bit further at the technicalities of the distinct temporalities of melody, harmony, and rhythm. In fact, we will see that the musical significances of these three dimensions overlap, but there remains a basic distinction in sense between each of these musical dimensions that is, furthermore, illuminative for the form of our experience more broadly.

A melody seems easily and obviously comparable to a line. It is a sequence of notes that goes from somewhere to somewhere. Indeed, jazz musicians often use the word "lines" when referring to the melodic

phrases played by a performer. It also seems fairly easy to compare melodic phrases to sentences. And, again, musicians often refer to the stringing together of musical phrases in a player's improvising as "telling a story." A sentence, like a line, is a sequence (this time of words) that again goes from somewhere to somewhere. One way in which the "sentence" image is helpful in a way that the "line" image is not is that the sentence is distinguished into different functional parts. Primarily, a sentence is a subject and a predicate, joined by the copula. And within that basic structure we distinguish the modifying roles of adjectives and adverbs from the more basic roles of nouns and verbs. Like a sentence, a melody is a temporal flow that evinces an organized structure of functional parts—beginning, development, embellishment, digression, ending—and that accomplishes a distinct movement from here to there. On the other hand, there is a way in which a musical phrase falls short of the articulation of language, and here the image of a line is helpful: the functional differentiation of its parts presents something like the form of a sentence, but there is no filling to the sentence—it does not say something definite *about* something beyond the music. Because it is so expressive, music often has been employed "programmatically" to convey the sense of a situation, and this is powerfully exploited in the use of music in advertising and in film sound tracks; nonetheless, the relationship of the music to what it is supposed to convey remains suggestive only, and there is no necessity to the linkage between apprehending the musical sense and recognizing the intended reference. A melody, ultimately, has direction and structure but no reference beyond itself and thus is in this sense more like a line than a sentence. Overall, we can summarize this by saying that the temporality of melody—that is, the form in which a melody organizes and embodies our experiential expectations for the resonating of past, present, and future—is the temporality of the unfolding of a *coherent sequentiality*. With rhythm, we encounter a different temporality, a different form of temporal organization.

Like the coherent sequentiality of melody, rhythm (in the narrow sense in which we typically use that term rather than in the comprehensive sense I am using as the generic name for all experiences of the propulsion of sense to fulfillment) also has an inherently directional, temporal character: it goes from somewhere to somewhere. But whereas the different moments of melody—the different notes—can be ever changing, can be ever different, there is an essential sameness to the sequentiality of rhythm: rhythm is fundamentally repetitive. A simple sequence of ever-changing punctuations never allows a basic rhythm to be *established*. A rhythm, however, is an established "beat," a smooth pattern of punctuation we expect to be repeated. A rhythm is a basic pulse and a basic meter—a groove—that is the temporal platform for the temporality of the melody, that is, *because* we are secure in our expectation of its repetition, the rhythm opens up a musical space within which or upon which a further musical sense (the melody) can be elaborated. Overall, then, rhythm has the temporality of *punctuated repetition.* Like rhythm and melody, harmony too has a unique temporality that stands in a functional relationship with the other two.

With melody, we have a diachronic temporal unity—a temporality of sequentiality. With rhythm, we have the different diachronic temporality of repetition. With harmony, the simultaneous playing of mutually resonating notes ("chords"), we have a further temporality. Harmony, though, is fundamentally a synchronic temporality rather than a diachronic one. This is because the temporality of harmony primarily involves simultaneity, that is, the notion of "at the same time" or, more exactly, "differences at the same time." There is, however, more to the temporal dimension of harmony, for harmony is not just static. Chords— the coherent sets of mutually resonating notes played simultaneously— are also parts of chord sequences, and in this way the temporal structure of harmony has some commonality with the structures of melody and rhythm. Like the melody, the chord sequence also is played out sequentially. Like rhythm, chord progressions themselves typically make up a larger form that is repeated. Furthermore, harmony will accept many melodies overtop of it, without changing its identity. But though it has these similarities to melody and rhythm, harmony remains a distinguishable domain of musical sense primarily because of its constitutive significance as the *simultaneity of the resounding* of sounds with each other. Harmony thus opens up a unique dimension of musical meaning that is characterized by a temporal structure of "at the same time," and it is thus primarily a temporality of simultaneity, but it also is characterized by a unique kind of sequentiality and a repetitiveness. It has a sequentiality, but not the same one as that of the melody, that is, we can hear the difference between the sequence of chords that establishes the qualitative environment for the sound and the changing sequence of melody notes that weaves a "narrative line" atop this setting; and it has a repetitiveness but, again, not the same one as that of the simple rhythm, that is, we can hear the difference between the harmonic pattern that is a shifting texture or coloring to the musical context and the rhythm that is a punctuated pattern of musical accents. Melody, rhythm, and harmony are these distinct temporalities, distinct forms of temporal significance, distinct and ever-present dimensions of musical sense as it reveals itself in terms of the forms of interconnection of past, present, and future. The music is accomplished through the integrated playing off of these different temporal significances against one another. This is the inherent polytemporality to the hearing of music.

These three "dimensions" of music each have a different temporality, but these different forms of temporality are all species of the more basic phenomenon of the fulfillment of sense in further sense. In other words, all draw on the same fundamental experience of directed resonance. All, in other words, elaborate aspects of the basic phenomenon of sense that I began by designating with the term *rhythm* (in the broad sense I have given to that word as the apprehension of the propulsion of sense toward its resolution in further sense). Focusing on these characteristics of music can be helpful for recognizing the dimensions of sense that characterize all experience, all perception of form. Our perception of rhythm in the broad sense reveals that our experience is always temporal, that is, it is always structured in terms of past (where we are coming from), present (where we are), and future (where we are going). What melody, harmony, and (what we usually call) rhythm show us, as we have seen, is that this temporality is itself multilayered. Just as space is always structured in the three dimensions of depth, breadth, and length, so is time always structured in terms of something like rhythm, harmony, and melody. Now that we have differentiated the basic temporal structures of these three, let us consider the basic musical "sense," the "meaning," of these temporalities, and then draw out their exemplary relevance for understanding experience in general.

Within a piece of music, the "rhythm," typically, is a basic groove or pulse: a repeated figure that provides the basic platform *upon* which the further dimensions of the musical piece are *established* and by which they are *supported*. The harmony (the "chord change") establishes a more complex structure of *resonance* within the piece that provides something like the *character* of the piece. The harmony is determinate, which means it has complexity and development within it, but it also remains self-same, even while accepting different melodies that can be played against it. The melody enacts the trajectory—the *narrative*—of the piece, differentiating forward and back, and introducing novelty and history into the piece. Of course, all these dimensions can be explained with greater complexity (and it is very much the work of music to explore them in their complexity), but something like this basic three-dimensionality—this threefold way of differently embodying and articulating the relations of past, present, and future—is present in all music and, indeed (as we shall soon see) in all temporal experience, that is, in all sense. In the musical piece, then, there is a polytemporality of nonprogressive repetition, resonant simultaneity, and sequential development, and this is, roughly, the polytemporality of *platform*, *character*, and *narrative*.

Within each of these polytemporal dimensions, the musical significance will be how the piece plays with the forms of temporal propulsion toward resolution. The music begins from the basic meanings of "platform," "character," and "narrative" and then establishes the experience of more subtle meanings. One can be "carried along smoothly" by the rhythmic platform, or one can be "abruptly thrown about," the harmonic character can be "rich" or "austere," the melodic narrative can be experienced as "revealing" what was lying in wait, or as "hinting" at what is to come, can be "digressing" or "embellishing" when not developing its main theme, and so on. These are the sorts of terms in which we experience the significance of the ongoing meaningful flow of a musical piece, and these are also the sorts of terms in which our perception of sense is always experienced.

Something like this threefold difference of "platform," "character," and "narrative" is reflected in my initial three visual examples: the dots suggest nonprogressive repetition, the segments of the geometrical pattern suggest something turned in upon and resonating with itself, and the image of the face suggests something like a complex, nonrepetitive narrative of a unique whole. Moving beyond those simple examples, we can see something analogous to the different musical possibilities for such meanings as "smooth transport," "rich texture," and "digression" that we just mentioned in the way a garden path invites us to stroll along it: we feel easily drawn into the flow of the path and feel ourselves engulfed by its luxurious richness; at the same time, the leisurely ways in which we pause to notice this or that do not hinder the ongoing trajectory. Something analogous to the musical "abruptness," "austerity," and "revelation," on the other hand, may well characterize my experience of my alcoholic father's arrival. He may be such that I experience his erratic behavior as always confronting me with new and sudden demands, and this may be the normal "rhythm" of being with him. He, too, like a challenging musical piece, may offer me little context for appreciating the character of his own situation, so he offers a rather "austere" "harmony." And successful navigation of the experience may repeatedly take the form of recognizing, "so that's what's happening," such that the "melody" of each experience strongly reveals, at certain points, where the main theme is developing. Indeed, getting to know my father or the garden requires apprehending these "musical" forms and learning to "dance" with them; my friend may be quite disconcerted by my father's behavior upon first meeting him, whereas I can easily flow with his music because I am familiar with it; or, again, your bringing an attitude of haste and single-minded directedness to our time in the garden may well preclude your apprehending this luxurious sense of itself that it makes available and may keep you from sharing the experience with me. In sum, our apprehension of anything is an ongoing temporal experience with its own characteristic rhythm, harmony, and melodic flow: there is a "musicality" to all experience.

Meaning, then, is inherently temporal, inherently "musical." All our experience evinces something like the flow of a melody—all we experi-

Meaning?

ence picks up on themes that were already developing and takes them in new directions, fulfilling certain anticipations while launching new ones. And this temporality is not singular in our experience: there can be many lines of melodic flow unfolding and developing concurrently. Further, the temporality of experience is not just the time of sequence, of before and after, but has also something of the temporalities of harmony and rhythm. Let us consider these temporal dimensions at the broadest level as they structure our everyday life.

First, there are the familiar, repetitive rhythms of day and night, hunger and drowsiness, the seasons, menstruation, and sexual arousal. These are, in short, the rhythms of *nature*. Our lives are always embedded in the temporality of nature, and that is a rhythmic temporality of repetition rather than a developmental temporality of melody. *We find our experience* swinging to these rhythms, and we operate within their pulsations, whether we like it or not. Indeed, this irremovable natural temporality may well conflict with the melodic temporality of our projects: our desire to see a friend may well be an unfulfilled anticipation because the need for sleep intervenes. Though we can in various ways manipulate these rhythms, those manipulations must themselves operate within the thresholds and parameters the natural rhythms enable.

In many ways, it is the harmonic temporality of our experience that is most interesting. I just noted the polymelodic form of our experience: the way that many lines of anticipation are enacted concurrently. These melody lines, though, are what we might call "figures" in our experience. Our experience also has "backgrounds," however, and these are fundamentally harmonic dimensions of meaning. I may concurrently be completing a telephone call, preparing a lecture, and getting ready for a lunch appointment. I am *in process* with all three: all three are currently flowing melodies. But all are enacted within my office, on campus, in the midst of my marriage, while I am employed, when my parents are alive. These last dimensions are the essential meaning-giving contexts within which my melodies are meaningful, but they are not themselves what my experience is currently "about." These contextualizing dimensions are a kind of grounding context, a context that remains and repeats itself throughout the developing time of melody. But unlike the repetitive rhythms of nature, these contexts are themselves *projective* or, loosely, cultural, that is, they are rooted in choices and plans we have made. Like harmonic progressions in a piece of music, they each have a path and a development of their own. Unlike the path and development of melody, however, these harmonic dimensions are not "at issue" for me right now. They are the assumed, regular medium within which the melodies of my daily life are meaningful. Like melodies, harmonies have a kind of narrative, a kind of sequentiality, but these harmonies are the structuring narratives that I have settled into, the grounding interpretations of my life to which I am habituated, rather than matters that are the subject of explicit attention and choice in my daily affairs. There is a rhythm of everyday life that is found in our embeddedness in nature, there are melodies found in our explicit, ongoing projects, and there is a harmony of everyday life found in our habits.

These harmonic dimensions, we also should note, can become thematic, can become the melodic center of my life. Whereas for many years I may have been settled in my position as a store manager and occupied myself with the daily affairs of managing the store while taking the fact of my employment for granted, I may become frustrated with my job and make changing it my primary concern, precisely because I am no longer happy with the context it offers for my other activities. In this case, my professional position has switched from being a matter of harmony to a matter of melody. Or, indeed, my job may itself be so engaging that it is always my primary concern: whereas for my colleagues, their positions as teachers may be a matter of routine that they barely notice as they carry out the ongoing melodic affairs of their friendships and family business, I may find the fact of my being a teacher fundamentally fulfilling and all-engrossing, and I may live out my daily activities *as* experiencing my enjoyment of my position, which is not so much harmonic as it is always the melody of my day. And, just as my experience is polymelodic, it also is polyharmonic. These different contextualizing dimensions can themselves conflict with each other—my family life and my career, for example, can run happily parallel at times but can each make demands that contradict those of the other at points of crisis. (Indeed, this is a situation in which these harmonic dimensions typically become melodies in our life.) They also have patterns of rising and falling that can be quite different, such that the family context is only prominently operative on weekends, while the career context harmonizes my weekdays, and, indeed, the different rhythmic patterns that are appropriate to these different harmonic dimensions can be coordinated, and they also can be sites of conflict.

From the smallest level of grabbing a doorknob or walking in a garden to the broadest level of the overall structure of a life, then, we can see that our experience is a dance, an apprehension of polytemporal musical forms. This is the structure of experience as such. Note, too, that the recognition of these rhythms, these resonances, is not primarily conceptual, nor is it typically explicitly self-conscious. We are bodily attuned to such epiphanies of sense, and our "dancing" receptiveness is typically habitual and automatic. The conceptual and the explicitly self-conscious are themselves developments of such attuned perception, and not vice versa. It is in this original making sense, this music to which we are bodily attuned, that all of our reality is given birth. We *emerge* in this matrix, this manifold, of rhythmic epiphany.

Wonder

We respond to the rhythmic cycle of the elements—the transmutation between earth, air, fire, and water. We are attuned to the rhythm of the day—dawn, morning, noon, afternoon, dusk, dark night. We resonate with the cycle of the seasons—summer, autumn, winter, spring. Within these rhythms, the melody of beginning-middle-end shows itself. The rhythm of exhaustion and recuperation within our own bodies and the melody of beginning-middle-end open the possibility of the harmonization of our actions in patience, planning, and cultivation, and also in haste, indulgence, expenditure, and so on. These senses are original epiphanies, neither created by our conceptualizing nor open to our refutation.

The compelling meaning—the *reality*—of patience and planning shows itself to us. The originative reality of the harvest cycle reveals itself to us. Behind them, there is the inexplicable nurturance of the sun that is the clarity of vision and of the earth that is the foundation of stability and consistency—these are two original senses, irreducible forms, that appear compellingly and guidingly for us. These are forms to which we are inexplicably attuned, and to which we owe everything. This can be said for the world of nature—*phusis*—in general. We only ever occur ourselves *within* the self-occurring realm of nature, and it is as already participant within the rhythm of nature that we find ourselves. The fertile earth, the sky that supplies nurturing warmth and clarifying light, and the self-sufficing rhythm of growth, death, and regeneration are not senses we invent or realities we make. It is only within their context that we occur. It is on their basis and through their resources that whatever "making" we do accomplish takes place. The Greeks called these "gods," and in an important sense these are gods indeed, that is, they are self-emergent powers to which we owe whatever we are: Gaea, Demeter, Zeus, Persephone.

The grape naturally ferments, and in the ingestion of its product we are overtaken by a new spirit—a spirit that clears for us a new appearance of ourselves, of our world, of our companions. In close contact with the body of another, our bodies and our perception are transfigured, overcome by the beauty of the other, drawn to bodily coupling. These, too, are original and originary epiphanies, encounters with self-emergent realities from which our experience takes form and to which we are answerable: Dionysus, Aphrodite, Eros. These irreducible, compelling realities *actually appear* in epiphanies that guide and nurture us and that we cannot control. It is these realities to which we must answer, and their very reality entails that we will be ruined if we fail to respect them.

We typically describe ourselves as "free" and "active." We talk about what we have "done" in our lives, and we list our "accomplishments." We are proud that we "think for ourselves" and that we "did it on our own."

The fundamental passivity

Yet all this activity is subtended by a more fundamental passivity. I did not make my ability to move; indeed, I did not make my ability to make! My ability to think is likewise (and we typically call it such) a "gift." All of our abilities—the very grounds on which we can be "active"—are given to us, that is, we find ourselves with certain abilities not of our own making. We often are most proud of ourselves because of our self-controlled self-possession, that is, our ability to be patient and reserved and to choose our words and actions carefully. But this patience is itself an attitude we *find* ourselves able to adopt. Again, we are proud for our insights, but insights *come to* us (and, indeed, they can be a burden we do not want). Wisdom, like the sun and like eros, is a guiding reality for us—Athena—and it is one that mixes in a complex way our receptivity and our agency.

I invoke the language of the gods (and I have chosen the Greek gods primarily because of my familiarity with them, and not as a statement of cultural preference) because this language reminds us of the originariness and givenness of the basic senses of our world and of the fundamental answerability that defines our experience. These forms—the earth, the sky, and the rest—are given, and as such they are obvious. Indeed, they define what it is to be obvious, for they are the very parameters of appearing. But precisely because they are thus obviously given, we take them for granted. We think and act on the basis of these senses, but we do not think to question them, to be puzzled by them, to wonder at them. Here, the second choral song from Sophocles' great tragedy *Antigone* (the so-called "Ode to Man," ll 332–75) is especially helpful. "Many are the wonders," says the chorus. The focus of their song is on the character of man—the most wonderful—but man is brought into focus through consideration of the other wonders, such as "Earth, oldest of gods," "the storming south winds," and "the races of savage beasts."

> Many are the wonders (*ta deina*), none
> is more wonderful than what is man.
> This it is that crosses the sea
> with the south winds storming and the waves swelling,
> breaking around him in roaring surf.
> He it is again who wears away
> the Earth, oldest of gods, immortal, unwearied,
> as the ploughs wind across her from year to year
> when he works her with the breed that comes from horses.
> . . .
> He has a way against everything,
> and he faces nothing that is to come
> without contrivance.

Only against death
can he call on no means of escape.
. . .

If he honors the laws of the earth,
and the justice of the gods he has confirmed by oath
high is his city; no city
has he with whom dwells dishonor
prompted by recklessness.
He who is so, may he never share my hearth! (trans. Lattimore)

There is much we could draw from a study of the details of this ode in its entirety, but our interest here is simply in noting the portrayal of our reality as that which exercises its wonderful (*deinos*, which means both great and terrible) power always within a context of other given wonders, to which we must bring the appropriate level of honor and respect. All of our accomplishments occur within and in the terms of this *given* world, through our *given* powers (most especially our "cunning" power to control nature by turning its powers against itself). That we are definitively constrained by the givenness is shown by the ineffaceability of our death, which marks the passivity of our existence: our existence is given us, and it will withdraw, neither by our own doing. The chorus calls upon man to honor these gods. Our task is to follow the lead offered by the chorus and to bear witness to the wonders of our everyday world.

My purpose in this chapter is ultimately to address the theme of method, and I invoke the language of gods to underline the idea that the method must be one of descriptive honesty. Our task is to present what shows itself as it shows itself, not to establish in advance a set of parameters to which our object must answer or a set of goals that we wish to accomplish. Such a method of description, such a witnessing to the epiphanies of sense, is in many ways simply an effort to adopt the stance of wonder that these "wonders" properly call for, and to recognize—perhaps for the first time—the shocking and miraculous dimensions of our everyday life that we normally take for granted. And, as we shall see, this noticing is not just an aesthetic exercise or a cultivation of feeling but is an education that will have the effect of reorienting us to the things of our world, primarily with respect to issues of responsibility. Our method of description, in other words, will ultimately lead us to something like ethics.

The Bodily a Priori

At one extreme, patterns of connected dots. At the other, Dionysus and Zeus. In the most immediate and familiar occurrence, music and dance.

Through all these illustrations I am trying to describe and present the phenomenon of *sense*. Sense has an irreducibly *given* character—we have to *find out* what it is. Sense is bodily and propulsive, that is, to sense is to receive in one's body the charge toward the further sense that would be fulfilling. Sense manifests itself as the partial presentation of a form, a compelling reality that appears by us but does not derive from us.

These features just mentioned are all quite important. (1) The *given-ness* of sense means we must always answer to how it shows itself, and therefore our highest science will be description rather than deduction. Indeed, in many ways it is the disciplines of history and poetry, rather than the disciplines of natural science and logic, that have the power to present most truly the nature of things. (2) The *bodily* character of sense indicates that we always exist in a state of tension, charged, between in-auguration and resolution, and that our perception will always be a matter of action, of doing. (3) That sense is an epiphany and a realization of *form* means both that we are always drawn beyond ourselves to bear witness to the miraculous births of unanticipated, compelling realities and also that any such realities can only be forms of engagement with our own bodily reality; in other words, the forms must answer to our possibilities for meaning at the same time as we must answer to the meanings thus informing us. (4) That presentation is always partial means that our experience is always grounded in something beyond itself, with which it is interwoven and toward which its partiality points. The epiphany is *of* a whole, *through* partial presentations. The forms are always available to be experienced again, or to be experienced otherwise; they are present as, but not exhausted in, their partial presentations.

With these four features in mind, I will characterize the forms of sense as the "bodily a priori." These forms are the chargedness of a bodily at-tunement to a directing sense that sets the arena of meaningfulness within which the determinate shapes of our lives are elaborated. It is the body's given opennesses, its determinate attunements that initiate us into the realms of sense. We will proceed now to investigate various aspects of such initiation; specifically, we will be considering initiation into the sphere in which we engage with the senses "I" and "We," and the various other mean-ings that are inherently involved in these notions of the person.

We will begin (chapter 2) with a consideration of the perceiving body and from here consider the basic form—the sense—of the world that exists for this body: we will see that it is a world of things, principles, marks, and other persons. Our primary relationship to this world is one of engagement—our own reality is interwoven with the reality of this world. In order to investigate what it is to be a person in terms of this context of the interwovenness of body and world, we will turn (chapter 3) to the child, for whom the reality of its own bodily self, the reality of things, and the reality of other people emerge together as an interwoven reality. It is this reality, the reality with which the child becomes familiar through family life, that opens the child beyond its initial field—a field in which self, world, and others are not antagonistically differentiated, a field in which play and creativity are primary—into the field of reality and responsibility, into the realms of communication (between self and others) and knowledge (of the world), and their attendant values of goodness, truth, and beauty (chapters 4 and 5).

2

♦♦♦

Ambiguity

On Metaphysics

What could be more obvious than that "there is"? What could be more obvious than reality? We only ever find ourselves as *already* involved with a world beyond us, and this "beyond" is that of which we fundamentally undergo epiphany. This "reality," though, this "there is," is fundamentally ambiguous. There is a multiple character to this "is" of which we have epiphany. We shall begin our investigation with the "is" that is the body—the "is" we find ourselves to be—and then move beyond that to the other forms of "is" with which the body is involved.

The Body

I can take my place at the meeting. I can catch the ball. I can reach the top cupboard and grasp the large serving dish I put there earlier. I can walk to your house. I can balance while standing on the bus. I can avert my eyes. I can greet him with a smile. I can hug you, embrace you with my whole body, caress and kiss you. Reaching, grasping, putting, walking, balancing, standing, looking, caressing: all of these are obviously inherently bodily activities. These are activities that shape and enact our engagement with the world, and all are developed from the specific character of our limbs and our physical powers. None of these engagements could be without a body, and their specific nature derives from our specific bodily nature.

As well as deriving its specific nature from the specific nature of my body, each of these activities is a meaningful engagement with the world beyond my immediate body. Each is an engagement of the body with something other than itself. Each also is a directed, prolonged activity and an initiation of change and development into the world. The very nature of the body is to act, and the very nature of action is always to be in relation to something beyond itself and to bring about some form of change through a temporal process characterized by the sorts of musicality we discussed in chapter 1. The living, acting body only exists as a temporal process of making a difference in the world.

Finally, each of these activities also is a meaningful reflection and enactment of my personality and my developed relationship with the world. In averting my eyes, I acknowledge the weight of your gaze, and I betray the history of my troubled dealings with you that is the harmony of our interaction. In taking my place at the meeting, I consent to accept the authority of the new administrator and inaugurate the next phase of my career. In walking to your house, I enact my commitment to healthy activity while making good on my promise to help you with your move. Reaching for the serving dish continues the rhythm and the melodic flow of the dinner party begun a half hour earlier. In our ways of acting, our whole identity is communicated and enacted; indeed, learning to see—and thence express—the whole personality through a simple gesture is very much the work of actors or of the clown, as described in Heinrich Böll's, *The Clown*:

> I observe all the ways of knocking off work with fanatical zeal: the way a workman puts his pay envelope in his pocket and gets on his motorbike, the way a broker finally lays down the telephone, puts his notebook away in a drawer and locks it, or the way the girl in the grocery store takes off her apron, washes her hands and fixes her hair and lips in the mirror, picks up her handbag—and away she goes, it is all so human. (93)

What the actor studies, and what we all unconsciously register and respond to in our dealings with our fellows, is the way of living that is communicated through our bodily actions. As Walt Whitman writes in "I Sing the Body Electric," "the expression of a well-made man appears not only in his face; / It is in his limbs and joints also . . . ; / It is in his walk, in the carriage of his neck" (ll 12–14). Our bodily acts are not isolated explosions of matter in motion but are the ongoing enactment of a life.

These activities are the stuff of our lives, the foundation of our relation with the world. They are inherently bodily—not acts of intellectual contemplation—and yet they are intelligent and meaningful. These actions reveal that our meaningful relation with the world is bodily, but also that our bodily relation with the world is meaningful. Our life in the world is a texture of actions, of bodily engagements. These are not the "vehicles" by which some disembodied, psychic meaning is transported about; rather, these actions are our life itself, its very enactment, realization, and articulation.

Just as these actions are not acts of contemplative intellect, so is the body itself not an inert material, powered by deterministic causality. The body itself is alive and dynamic, and it is the site and source of meaning, initiative, and development. The body that *I am* cannot be adequately comprehended by chemistry or physics. These sciences may certainly offer useful approaches to objects, but they reduce the dimensions of reality that they will accept as real to a very narrow set of measurable properties. The living body, however, is a reality that exceeds these reductive terms; it cannot be properly understood by a science that does not have as its terms of analysis such notions as "meaning," "development," "initiative," and so on.

Our body is a material specificity, but its reality is fundamentally found in its powers—its ability to be open to epiphany—not in the assemblage of isolated physical actualities studied in mechanics, chemistry or anatomy. The body is the hand, not as quantities of skin and bone but as *flesh*, as the magical capacity to touch and to grasp. The hand's reality is grasping power, feeling power. This is the character of the body as a whole: the body is a material specificity, but a specificity the very nature of which is to open up—open ourselves up—to what is beyond it. The body's powers are powers of self-transcending, of opening, of learning. As a body, I look *at* something, I balance *within* a larger world, I reach *out*, I grasp an *other*. These essential, definitive bodily powers can themselves only be defined—can only be understood—by essential reference to a reality beyond the body's immediate determinacy. This is the nature of the body: it is the power we are to be in a world. The body's reality is not exhausted by itself, by its own actuality, but is always beyond itself. The body is our power to bear witness to epiphany.

By its nature, then, the body is double. It is itself, but it is itself only by being beyond itself. It is only as self-transcending. Its reality is *ecstasis*, standing outside of itself in the revelation of an epiphanic reality. Our body is our being thrown into the world beyond, but "thrown" not as a temporal sequence but as a definitive form: we are "always already" thrown outside of ourselves. Our body is our always being already thrown beyond ourselves, and yet it is equally our root in reality. Like the plant, we can grow into the larger surrounding atmosphere, but we cannot survive being uprooted. The body is our being thrown beyond ourselves, but it is equally our inherence in a specificity—an absolute, irremoveable, noneffaceable specificity. As a body, I am always out there, in the world I can grasp and feel, out there in the reality of the world of things epiphanically revealed to me. But I am also always here, right here, where I am. The body is this tension, this ambiguity, of throwing me into a world there by rooting me absolutely in a unique specificity here. Like Janus, the two-faced Roman god of gates and doorways, beginnings and endings, the body is inherently double.

This character of the body as a whole of opening me to the shared reality of a world in itself but doing so only by putting its own distinctive mark

Perspective

upon this opening, this character as "a perspective," equally characterizes the various specific powers and aspects of the body. Reaching, grasping, balancing, looking: these are the names of our primitive bodily engagements with the world. They also are names upon which we rely to designate and express far more sophisticated engagements: I grasp what you are saying, I reach my career goal, I seek balance in the different aspects of my life, I look for a partner. These uses of "grasp," "reach," "balance," and "look" are not empty or discardable metaphors: they express, rather, that our most sophisticated and rich activities are developments within the parameters of engagement first opened up for us by our immediate bodily powers. This also indicates that the meaning of "grasp" is not itself exhausted in its first, immediate, and primitive manifestation in the simple functioning of the hand; what these "metaphors" show is that the meaning-potential revealed in that initial, immediate opening is itself capable of elaboration and development beyond that inaugural occurrence. We grasp the ball with our hands, and we grasp the meaning of a difficult lecture, we balance upon the earth, and we balance our conflicting commitments: the specific powers of our body are all self-transcending powers that open up parameters of interaction that grow beyond themselves into richer, more sophisticated, more universal powers. These primitive bodily experiences of these powers open us up into the realm of those powers as such and allow us to grow into their reality: by virtue of our enhandedness, we have an access into the meaning of "grasp" as such, as an inexhaustible type of possible significance. Equally, these primitive bodily powers forever affix their stamp to the parameters of meaningfulness for us: our grasping will become ever more sophisticated, but it will always be grasping, always the kind of revealing of significance that is possible for a being who enters reality by way of our bodily specificity, our enhandedness.

This is our bodily nature. We are thrown beyond ourselves into a world by virtue of our absolute rootedness in a specificity from which we can never distance ourselves. Our body is this perspective, this determinate openness. As such, the body throws us beyond ourselves into a reality not just our own, into reality as such, but it does so only and always by stamping that opening with its own specificity. The body is a set of self-transcending powers that open us to meaningfulness—to creativity, initiative, and the epiphanic revelation of emergent realities that exceed their preconditions—and yet these revelations, these rhythms, always bear the mark of the bodily specificities with which they resonate, in whose matrix they were born. The body is a material meaningfulness and a meaningful materiality, a determinateness that is ambiguously specific and universal, ecstatic and inherent, itself and beyond itself. All of our meanings are bodily, and this bodily ambiguity marks the meaning of all of our reality.

Let us turn to this opening onto the world—to the nature of perception and understanding.

Perception

Our perceptual life is our unavoidable thrownness into the world of things. We find ourselves simultaneously engaged with and detached from things, and we find things themselves simultaneously attached to and detached from other things.

Things have a density; they are a viscous congealedness of reality that enforces a set of determinacies and limits upon all else. They evince an irrefutable oneness and autonomy, a realization of reality not subordinate(able) to any other. Each thing is an "each," a substantiality unto itself: the thing is not "from" some other reality that is an independently existing source but *is itself real*—the thing is the very happening of reality. Each thing thus stands as a kind of absolute, self-defining and authoritative: it is a kind of metaphysical magnet, sucking reality and meaning unto itself, expressing its reality through a multiplicity of viscous, vibrant senses—fuzzy texture, luminous red, sharp edges.

These viscous, vibrant senses are not dull properties but sites of life and power: I experience the white page as inviting inscription, the tender flesh as inviting caress, the bright eyes threatening condemnation. All things are like this page, this flesh and these eyes, in that they invite our involvement, through which involvement the nature of the things is revealed but never exhausted. Things are wild, each a wilderness, a rich jungle life. Our perceptual life is our life in this wild geography of verdant senses, each drawing us farther into a swarming life of pressures, textures, and viscosities in which we can never fail to be immersed.

The absorbing attractiveness of the sensuousness of the unique thing is well known to children. As Böll writes in *The Clown*, "In a child's life, there is a greatness in the banal, it is strange, random always tragic" (93). This enthusiasm for the strange, tragic richness of things also is familiar as the motivation for the sort of "naturalistic" exploration so well portrayed by Annie Dillard in *Pilgrim at Tinker Creek*; Dillard engaged in an intense, enthralled observation of the intimate details of a natural setting, sometimes, for example, by lying for hours on her stomach while observing a tiny spot on the creek. The hypnotic, absorbing attraction of things also is seen in the protagonist's experience of observing the reflection of his own face, again, in *The Clown*:

A clown, whose main effect is his immobile face, must keep his face very mobile. I used to always stick out my tongue at myself before I began my exercises, so as to get quite close to myself before

I could withdraw from myself again. Later on I stopped doing that, and without any tricks whatever just stared at myself, every day for half an hour, until finally I wasn't there at all: as I have no narcissistic tendencies, I often came close to going mad. I simply forgot it was me whose face I was looking at in the mirror. (130)

Things always offer themselves as such invitations for infinite exploration and as Böll's protagonist notes, abandoning oneself to the parameters of the unique "world" of the thing (here the reflection of one's own face) entails letting go of the parameters of the larger world of our experience within which the thing normally resides, that is, to give into the thing is to court "madness." (Something similar happens with words: we can respond to them as inconspicuous carriers of an intellectual meaning, as we typically do when we read, or we can get caught up in their sensuous specificity, as when we are captivated by a rhyme.)

And yet, though we are always wrapped up with things, we are never simply immersed. We always have, hovering above our involvement, an atmosphere of detachment from these things. We are not solely immersed: we also *notice* our immersion, and this space of noticing allows us breathing space, a freedom of movement among things, rather as the bird, though an animal of the land, can use the air to relieve momentarily its attachment to the earth and exercise some guidance over its points of contact. As Maurice Merleau-Ponty says of our power to pay attention in his *Phenomenology of Perception* (29), "Attention, therefore, as a general and formal activity, does not exist. There is in each case a certain liberty to be acquired, and a certain mental space to make the most of." We are never simply detached, never simply alien to the world, but have, rather, access to some power to control for ourselves how we will deploy our resources. Experience does not just happen *to* us, but also *for* us, and this relation of "for" defines a zone of differentiation between perceiving and the very world that perceiving is "about."

Our own character as immersed-detached is thus the *folding of the perceptual world over onto itself* in the double stance of *identification with* and *noticing of* it. We *experience* the world, appreciate it, allow its reality to be recognized for the reality that it is. By virtue of being a "fold," we give to things their outside: we give them the arena within which they can be registered and established; we let them live an independent life by not allowing all of reality simply to be immersed in itself as the dark night, the absolute black hole, of nonperception. Our detachment enables theirs.

With this detachment, then, comes the *field* of reality. In the opening of this field, the clearing of a shared world, a reality beyond the thing is realized in the thing: the thing is both itself—discrete, unique—and beyond itself with other things and in other things. The thing is a thing by

Field

sharing reality with the other things with which it resonates, the other things that echo its significance in and through their own metaphysical magnetism, their colors, their offerings and threats. The things effect a chorus in which reality is manifest as the harmony of their mutual echoings. As many organisms weave themselves together in a natural ecosystem, so do things in their very being weave together to produce a field of being, a context and texture of reality, a form that exceeds that of the thing itself, though rooted within it, a *world*. This exceeding form, however, is not just a product or an aggregate of the things, for the very way in which they reveal it through themselves is *as* an autonomous reality itself. Things, in other words, announce through themselves their embeddedness in and dependence on a further "absolute," this "world" to which they belong. Like the power that is self-defined but rooted for us in the specific bodily paths through which we were initiated into it, there is a reality as such—"being" itself—that is never exhausted by the actual things through which it is announced, but that is always uniquely emergent from them in their determinateness and specificity. It is our ecstatic, self-exceeding selfhood that enables this ecstasis of things. The ambiguous structure of our self-exceeding selfhood finds its analogue in the reality of the thing that both holds itself in determinate isolation and extends beyond itself into a collectively constituted field of reality, itself enabled by the detachment that constitutes our own ambiguous immersion in things.

This ambiguity within things rebounds back upon us and the ambiguity within perception that enabled it. The draw of the thing—the attractive, "magnetic" force it impresses upon us *to perceive it*—contains the ambiguity of the thing itself. The pressure to perceive the thing—the chargedness in our bodies called forth by the rhythm of things—is as much the pressure to perceive the interweaving of things as it is the pressure to become immersed in the unique, singular isolation of each. Things draw us to perceive them beyond their singularities in their togetherness. This is the draw of understanding, of *com*-prehension, *con*-ception. Hence the enthusiasm of the young naturalist in *Pilgrim at Tinker Creek* that is as much directed toward noting relationships and establishing explanations for the interrelations of things as it is drawn into observational absorption in the uniqueness and sensuous specificity of the thing; hence the enthusiasm of Ishmael, the narrator of Herman Melville's *Moby Dick*, for whom the whole of reality seems implied in the lineaments of the body of the whale. Our perceptual life itself, then, has the double character of being drawn to things in their singularity and being drawn beyond them to their community and commonality. Our perceptual life has a double sense that responds to the duplicity of the reality of things.

Understanding, then, is as original and as revelatory of reality as is our being in the thrall of thingly sensuousness. Understanding is "dancing" to the epiphany of the larger form of reality that shows itself through the things of our world. The appropriately compelling force of this epiphany of the "intelligible" (principles, grounds, etc.) is often so overwhelming that we assign to it exclusive weight for determining the nature of the real. We must recall, though, that this epiphany itself emerges only in the context of things, which themselves appropriately offer epiphanies of their own metaphysical autonomy—epiphanies that are no less compelling and no less irreducibly present in experience than the epiphanies of understanding. The epiphanies of sensuous thinghood remain no less authoritative, no less real, than those of understanding. Our perceptual life is thus irremediably characterized by the tension between thingly perception and understanding.

And, indeed, inasmuch as this duplicity in things is itself enabled by that opening up of the field that comes with our detachment, our perceptual life is impressed with the magnetic force of this detachment itself, that is, we are drawn to self-perception. Our own character attracts us to itself, whether in narcissistic self-absorption, in self-interpretive insight, or in wonder. That my experience of the world is *my experience of* the world is no less compelling an epiphany than that it is my experience *of the world*, and this dimension within all experience offers as inexhaustible a domain for further exploration as do the inexhaustible domains of things and understanding. In our experience we live the tension of objective versus subjective, as well as that of perception versus understanding.

Things, in sum, burst forth with singular sense as engulfing forms, while simultaneously resonating with the realities of other things and echoing the reality of our own detachment, thereby throwing us beyond ourselves by the same magnetic power that draws us into their heart.

Attitude

Our immersed-detached character, manifest as perceptual life, always has a style. Our immersion is a feeling: we are affected by the things of our world. Part of the nature of being is that it is that about which we cannot fail to have an emotional attitude. Being affects us, matters to us. We care about it. This means that our normal perception of immersed familiarity is always charged this way or that about the situation as a whole. Our immersion is not just the fact of ontological inseparability but the *experience* of having a mood about things, the experience of *feeling* the impingement of things upon our reality. In this way, things again reveal their nonindependence from us by bearing as their very texture our own affectivity. Both individual things and things-as-a-whole can impinge upon us as inviting or repulsive, energizing or depressing, sparkling or dull, tedious or vibrant. These feelings are our original openings onto things, our original attunements, and it is within the possibilities here opened up that our different perceptual attitudes are developed.

The different attitudes we take up in our lives correspond to different sides of the perceptual field. Different attitudes realize and reveal thingly reality in its different facets. Some attitudes are more responsive to making room for the deeper grounds that are manifest through the fabric of things, some are more responsive to dwelling in the richness of specific, local settings, and some are more responsive to bringing forth the distinct character of one's own immersion-detachment. Our stances to a greater or lesser degree are one-sided in that they reveal certain facets of our situation while denying the reality or weight of the others. Let us explore these different attitudes.

In our everyday behavior, we move through our world—through our days—easily engaging with and drawing upon our network of familiar things. In our habitual use of things, we realize our immersion in them, our easy identification with the reality they proffer. We comfortably take root in our rooms, our families, our streets, our garments, our friends, and we make our lives simply the final connection in a circuit through which a single current flows. Our *immersion* in things and their mutual re-sounding here dominates reality as we live it. Here, things are the stable scaffolding of the harmonic dimension of our experience. What is ignored here is our *detachment*, and also the *exclusive* reality claimed by each thing. Indeed, this ability to ignore the demands of each thing and to ignore the pressure of our own detachment is crucial to our being able to settle, and to make a home for ourselves—both in the broad sense of becoming comfortable in how we inhabit the world and in the narrow sense of setting up a place to live. This, our epiphany of the world as home, could be construed as a witnessing to the Greek goddess Hera, as the goddess, primarily, of family life. In this happy absorption in our familiar abode, we may easily never notice what is always on the table, the cracks in the walls, or the dust accumulating in the corner, precisely because our attitude is directed away from the demands of such individualities and toward the unchanging and unchallenging uniformity of our own comfortable space (perhaps like Odysseus's attitude for many years on Circe's island, or like the attitude of Dickens's character Barnaby Rudge, who constantly allows his attitude to be drawn away from engagement with emergent difficulties). Our experience can be otherwise, however, and we can move away from our normal experience of a dynamic balance of richness and clarity within experience to an experience that is more melodically absorbed in its richness or to an experience that is more melodically intent upon clarification.

The epiphany of the rich uniqueness of the thing that contrasts with the attitude of our everyday harmonization with the world is found in one's thrilled absorption in the feel of the lollipop in one's mouth, in the wonderful taste of the beef Wellington, in the charming magic of this evening with a new friend, in the longing for those lips, in the excited desire to return to this novel. This power of the thing to break us out of our comfortable attitude is seen in the first chapter of William Faulkner's *The Sound and the Fury* in the description of the experience of the mentally retarded Benji. In Benji's experience with flowers in particular, the experience of absorption in the thing seems clear: giving him a jimson weed to hold immediately has the effect of pacifying him and drawing him out of whatever frame of mind he was otherwise in. We often have similar experiences, whether in minor events that distract us from our activities, or in grand events in which a strong experience with an individual thing can lead us to reconsider our usual ways of behaving. Perhaps it is such epiphanies of the hypnotic, intoxicating character of the particularities of the individual and the local that lie behind some aspects of the Greek recognition of the god Dionysus (though the experience of Dionysus, as the Greeks typically understand it, is inherently communal; indeed, the general tone of Hindu mythology seems better to capture this notion of the magic of the singular than does Greek mythology). When we undergo such experiences, our perception is focused away from the easy common circuit of comfortable immersion and on the all-consuming magnetism of the reality of this thing. In such experiences, a real form is clearly revealed in a way that it cannot otherwise be in our attitude of quotidian comfort. And yet this unique focus on the single thing itself denies the resonance within the thing of all the others and suppresses the reality of our own detachment. In our absorption in the individual thing, we lose sight of the structural demands of our normal life, and we "forget ourselves." Indeed, this absorption by things can be a great relief to us, as particular places or things can offer us an escape from our normal engagement with the world. For Mrs. Bentley, the narrator in Sinclair Ross's novel *As For Me and My House*, her walks along the railroad tracks allow her to "lose" herself and her normal focus on the troubles in her married life; for Stacey, the protagonist of Margaret Laurence's *The Fire-Dwellers*, her experience of an unfamiliar cabin offers her the resources to step out of her married life and participate in sexual activity she could not otherwise harmonize with her life. There is an epiphany of the absorbing uniqueness of things, and the "dance" that bears witness to this epiphany is not just a "contemplative" activity but is a whole mode of comportment, a way of engaging oneself with the world.

In our sciences and in our practical planning, we try to understand our world, and here we see the attitude intent upon clarification that is the other contrasting attitude to our everyday complacency with things. Here, in our attitude of explicitly intending to understand, we make manifest our detachment, our ability to stand apart from immersion in the windowless isolation of the thing and to comprehend the larger field as such. The stance of understanding further focuses on the incontrovertible commonness of things, their intrinsic participation in a shared reality. In understanding there is again an epiphany of form, a unique realization of the nature of things, for understanding bears witness to the nonisolatability of things from each other and from our folded-over nature as noticers—*as witnesses.* And yet understanding, for all of its revelatory truth (perhaps the revelation of Apollo), suppresses the recognition of the irreducibility of the uniqueness of singular realities, suppresses the recognition of the rootedness of this detachment in an irremoveable immersion, and suppresses the recognition of the primacy and originariness of bodily specificity.

There is no escape from these multiple attitudes—each is an epiphany of form, emergent from the very nature of our bodily, perceptual reality. They each—like things—offer an originative, verdant specificity that is simultaneously discrete and resounding with its involvement with the others. We are drawn to each of these attitudes, though we often, as individual persons, have a predilection for one of these epiphanies of reality over the others, rather as Socrates says, in the *Phaedrus* (247a), that each soul is naturally in the train of one or the other of the gods. Like all the forms of the bodily a priori, these inexhaustibles, these forms—these rhythms in the broad sense—are given; all are naturally emergent from the inexhaustible "chiasm" of body-world. They are the articulations of the sense of our lives and are both its irremovable structures and its avenues for growth.

We have seen three fundamental attitudes that derive from the interweaving of the ambiguous nature of things and our own ambiguous nature as immersed-detached. In addition to these overall attitudes of (1) everyday living, (2) perceptual absorption, and (3) scientific understanding, there is a fourth stance of note. This is the stance of perception via resonance, via the adoption of the *stance* of self-emergent autonomy. We can, that is to say, ourselves make *ourselves* "metaphysical magnets," and, like a thing, absorb reality through our self-expression in contagious, demanding determinacy. This fourth attitude is the attitude of expression or art.

Marks

The music appears only by calling forth from us the dance. While the dance is expressive and creative, it seems overall to have a receptive character, a sense of being led. Sometimes, though, we are called upon to be more active, more creative, in order to allow a form to appear. In enthusiasm, for example, we can feel impelled to shout, "Look!" or, in danger, "Look out!" Such situations call for a greater constructive intervention. This is the emergence of language. Language is the rhythmic reception that *establishes*, that leaves behind itself a transformed world. The dance is fleeting, but the song resonates into the future.

As with rhythm, harmony, and melody, song and dance merely emphasize different aspects of the same fundamental phenomenon: engaged attunement. To be attuned is to be engaged always in reception as creative expression. But whereas I have used rhythm and dance to emphasize our receptive "called-upon" nature, I will use song and language to emphasize the creative, self-establishing, "active" aspect of our nature.

As the music can call us, irresistibly, to move rhythmically, so do other situations call from us expression. To witness the imminence of a collision between a friend and an automobile is to cry, "Look out!" Perhaps one cannot resist the pressure to say "hello" to the person one passes on a lonely avenue. Perhaps one cannot resist expressing one's disgust at the scene just witnessed. These and many others are situations we live *as* the need to speak.

In these situations, speaking feels like the release of a great tension, something like the opening of a dam that allows the flooding waters to pour forcefully down a proper, constructive path instead of destructively and arbitrarily swelling and crashing, or instead of simply dissipating in a lost moment. Speaking channels these forces, these pressures, and makes them into something determinate as it simultaneously realizes and guides them. It is akin to the lightning rod that entices the electricity to channel itself through it and to resolve the tension between the earth and the sky that is manifest in the brewing of the storm.

When we express, we establish a determinacy. I make a mark, a sound, or, like Jacob, set up a stone (*Genesis* 28:11–19). In each case, the expression is specific. Yet with this determinacy I crystallize and show forth the great realm of meaning that I experience as trying to appear, trying to be realized. This mark has within it a complexity and depth of resonance akin to that of the thing.

The mark is, of course, a thing—a determinate reality actually existing in the world. Whatever characterizes the possibilities of our perceptual life must surely likewise characterize the possibilities of the mark. But *as mark* the mark assumes a different reality from that of the thing. Properly to be designated a mark, it is required that this "thing" be an epiphany. The mark qua mark must be the resonating of a form, the portal by which a new reality—a reality beyond the thingliness of the mark—enters into our field and impresses itself into our bodies. The mark is the conduit by which a new rhythm is conducted into us.

New words spoken in love evince this magic clearly. The charge that builds up within two people (or more), that presses upon the individuals through all the things of their worlds, that rises up inside their bodies, the urgency that constantly threatens that it must be embraced or wasted— this charge is suddenly materialized in the words of love that usher in a new reality: the reality of the shared experience of love, the reality of a bond. It is clearly the words that allow the feelings to be realized, and it is their efficacy that fabricates the new world of shared intimacy. We feel in such words their creative power. We feel it as we speak them and as we hear them. These words do not describe something that was already available: they do something. They are the bridge between us that brings us together into a new reality that did not preexist the words and that neither partner could produce alone. The words bear witness to and enact the epiphany of a reality: love. And the new reality inaugurated through these words is not a single entity *within* the parameters of our already existing world but is a new world, that is, the reality of our loving bond is now something that we live within, something within which the other things of the world are housed. Using the language of music that we introduced in chapter 1, we can say that the mark initially appears to be simply an element in the ongoing narrative flow of melodic life, but in fact its effect is to transform the very harmonic structure of a situation. Through the mark a new reality is inaugurated, and we subsequently live within the epiphany made available through the mark.

This is the magic of the mark: to summon into being a new reality, not explicable in terms of what preceded, not defined in terms of the parameters of the preceding world, and not equal to the thingly character of the mark. This is another a priori of our world that we discover through experience, namely, the epiphanic character of the mark.

We have words called forth from us, as in the case of the impending accident, and these words can themselves creatively usher in a new reality, as in the words of love. Yet these are not the ways we often experience our words. Far from unique and transformative, words typically pour from our mouths as if meaninglessly. We pay little heed to what we say, for the words are just the currency of daily life—trivial, decorative, or utilitarian. And yet here too these expressions are not nothing. They are fundamentally the means by which we navigate our dealings with our fellows. As bat and glove are the requisite means for navigating the baseball, words are the means for navigating our daily lives with others. With our words— even the trivial words of daily chatter—we direct flows, open gates, terminate trajectories, engineer new couplings. And all of these realities—new friendships, renewed contracts, terminated conversations, rearranged plans—are realities that exist only in the realm of the word, that is, they are all variant modes of the form of reality ushered in by the mark.

These quotidian dealings are not unique and transformative, but regular. Our words in such dealings navigate and maneuver within the terms of an already established world—they do not seek to revolutionize. This is possible because marks, like things, bear, beyond their self-defining uniqueness, the resonance of and promise of integration with others. The transformative mark brings to light a new reality, but for that very reason also, then, it offers that new reality as a field within which to operate. Transformative words take us to a new reality but, by virtue of their bridging, they precisely inaugurate the gradual integration of the new with the old, that is, they set up communication. The creative expression carries within it the promise of a coherent language, a *system* of articulation and interpretation.

Each unique, originative mark, then, has the structure of revealing itself to be merely an instance of a larger system of articulation of the reality to which it bears witness. The mark, that is, is unique, in that through its singular determinacy it inaugurates a world. And yet the very nature of this world—this reality—that it allows to appear is such as to be articulable otherwise, thus relegating its own determinate opening—the artwork, the originative mark—to the status of one among many, a mere carrier of a message rather than a creator. Here we see the same ambiguity as that evinced by the body and the thing. On the one hand, the emergent meaning is uniquely dependent on the specificity of its origination. On the other hand, this meaning, once originated, shows itself to exceed the specificity of its beginning.

Just as the multiple facets of perception give rise to a multiplicity of one-sided attitudes revealing its form, so too the multifaceted character of the mark gives rise to a multiplicity of attitudes in relation to the mark. We can engage with the mark in a creative epiphany, or we can navigate with marks. Because it is also a thing, we can perceive it or study it. From these attitudes come poetry, conversation, dictionaries, and linguistics.

Lurking within all the facets of the sign, though, is a single anchoring point. In all its forms, the mark is a reality within the reality of the folding of reality onto itself, that is, within the reality that is detachment within immersion. Marks, in other words, are only realities within the world of perception. They are realities in which we as percipient bodies are necessarily involved. Further, they are realities specially defined by the reality of the bond among percipient bodies: marks are realities of communication for those who recognize one another. What lurks within all marks, then, is other people.

Others

We have been engaged in metaphysics. We are discerning the ways of being that characterize reality. This is the metaphysics that emerges

from the world of bodily involvement, or what I earlier called the bodily
a priori.

In looking at the body, the thing and the mark, we have already discovered myriad insufficiencies in the traditional metaphysics that presumes a thing simply and unambiguously "is" itself ("A = A"), that is, in
the traditional concepts that have been developed for characterizing the
aforementioned realities. We have already seen the need for a metaphysics of suggestion and promise, a metaphysics of ambiguity, of immersion and detachment as the single nature of the fold, of the
self-subordinating dynamism of the epiphanic mark, and so on. In investigating the mark, we have found the pervasiveness of others within this
reality, and so we turn now to the new metaphysics of the other.

The form of experience is "receiving a call." We answer to the call of
form. The call—the rhythm that beckons us to dance and sing—comes *from
reality*. It occurs *for us*. But our answer is an action—a determinate change
within the world. Our answer, that is, is public: when we answer, we answer
to others. Just as reality occurs for us, so do we experience ourselves as before
others: we are noticed. Further, paralleling our own double structure as immersed-detached, our others are similar foldings of reality onto itself, and
thus the other whom we are before is not simply detached and alien. The
other and I are mutually immersed—in each other, in reality.

Like the mark, the other is a thing—a body in the world (like myself)—
but the other has a unique character *as other* that differs from the thing of
simple, perceptual life. It is in the face of the other that I feel humiliated, it
is another I can love, it is the other for whom I can feel respect and admi-
ration, and most of all it is the other with whom I can share language and
thereby the epiphany of reality.

Other people—ways in which reality is "folded otherwise"—have us
before themselves. They are to us the epiphany of *the perspective upon ourselves*, a perspective that we can never occupy. Any thing is a reality unto
itself and seems therefore to offer us the promise of a reality beyond ourselves. At the same time, however, the thing itself exists only within the
field opened up by our own detachment. Thus there lurks within our
perception the recognition that reality happens here, where I am. To a
degree that the thing by itself cannot accomplish, the other person, however, offers us the epiphany that reality happens somewhere else. Whatever claim we ourselves might have to be the site, the other appears to us
as having a comparable claim. Inasmuch as we experience the other as
the one *we* are before, the other is for us the epiphany of a reality for
which we are an epiphany of reality, that is, we manifest to the other the
primacy of our "here"; inasmuch as we experience the other as the one
we are *before*, the other is for us the epiphany of ourselves *as* not the locus
of the real.

Here is another great tension and ambiguity within our experience. We face simultaneously the overwhelming evidence of our own centrality and primacy in the world and the evidence that another has an equal claim to the same status. We ourselves are manifest to ourselves *both* as absolutely unique *and* as an example of a type, that is, as one among others. In our study, we recognized in the thing the shift from its absolute uniqueness to its subordination to a reality that exceeds its individual reality; through the other person, we have an *experience* of this shift, that is, through the other my reality experiences a challenge to its own uniqueness. We will never "settle" the ambiguity of immersion and detachment that characterizes our perceptual life, and similarly we will never "settle" the issue of our unique primacy versus our "species" membership with regard to other people. These are the given forms of our life. They define the terms for possible sense rather than offer specific experiences, which might be exchanged for some other. This tension of ourselves vis-à-vis others is lived *as* the experience of responsibility, the experience of erotic attraction, the experiences of sharing, competition, and antagonism. Love, duty, conflict, communication—these are realities. They are forms of sense that appear to us bodily. The world we live in—a world with other people—will always be a world in which questions of conflict, love, and duty will be pertinent and compelling.

Our World

We have thus sketched out the form of our world, the epiphanic parameters of the bodily a priori. We are ambiguously rooted in reality. We are immersed in a body, things, signs, and other people and detached from them all. Each of these is itself an ambiguous reality that simultaneously draws reality up into itself and bleeds out into the rest. We are drawn to society and understanding—to universality and abstraction—and also to locality and even to isolation. All of these realities are so many pressures, so many charges, so much music. Having completed this initial sketch of the elements of our world, we can now turn to a more detailed study of *how* these different elements are involved with each other in the emerging process of the developing life of the person. In identifying the permanent elements that are the scaffolding of our world, that punctuate the real, we have found something like the platforms upon which our lives are mounted. Having thus mapped out what we could call the basic "metaphysical rhythms" of our world, we can turn now to consider the harmonic textures into which they are woven and the melodic narratives that are elaborated through and atop them. We can now consider, that is, the rich meaningfulness of personal identity and (inter)personal life that is inaugurated within these parameters that constitute our world.

3

◆◆◆

Learning and Insight

On Epistemology

We have considered the basic form of reality, the basic form of the "what" of our experience. Now we turn to something like the "how" of it: how we (come to) apprehend this "what." Typically, approaches to this question have begun from assuming that our detached character is our sole reality, and from assuming that reality is not ambiguous; such approaches have tried to capture this "how" of our experience by developing a model of "knowledge," according to which we are self-contained "minds" who "represent" a world based on "information" we receive. By remembering the ambiguity of things and the ambiguity of our own immersed-detached character, we will see that the "how" of our experience is much more a matter of *involvement* than it is of "knowledge" in the narrow, representational sense typically given to that term. Also, inasmuch as we are here studying the "subjective" side of experience—focusing on the "how" of the experiencing rather than on the "what" of the experienced—this chapter is also an investigation of the "who" of our experience. We are witnesses to epiphany, and in the first two chapters, we have begun to grapple with this our identity as perceivers. We will now see our identity as perceivers to be the identity of "knowers" in a rich sense of insightful engagement, to be "family members," to be "individuals," and to be "witnesses." To see this expansion and articulation of our identity as perceivers, we thus turn now to the description of the dance by which we come to inhabit the world of our developed lives.

Insight

Understanding is not an error. It is not a fantasy. It is not a vain hope. Understanding is a reality. We are beings capable of insight. Insight is epiphany, the revelation of form. We do have the experience of coming to *see* the *nature* of things. This happens when the secret plot of a novel suddenly comes clear, and we can say, "Now I see what was going on," or "Now I get what's happening." This happens when we finally grasp the point the professor has been trying to make. Something analogous happens when, after repeated listenings to some complex orchestral piece, or to an unfamiliar new musical style, one suddenly "hears the music"; one might say, "Now I hear it," where formerly one heard many notes without much sense. One can similarly come to recognize the style of a painter or a period, such that one might say, "Now I see what her work looks like," that is, one comes to recognize the "look" of a Cézanne painting or of Renaissance architecture. In each case, there is a kind of inductive practice at work: multiple encounters with the immediate appearance of the things or work, followed by an intuition—an insightful grasp—of a reality beyond this immediacy. Further, this "reality beyond" is itself *given in experience as* the truth—the real reality—of the thing in question. It is not a prejudice or a presumption that leads us to count this "reality beyond" as the truth; rather, this is its epiphanic form. We witness the epiphany of this reality *as* the principle, the source, of that with which we are engaged. We are beings who comport ourselves in relation to principle: we are witness to principles as principles. To see the principle is to have the total situation itself "cleared" in a new way.

In these cases of "inductive" epiphany, our access to an inexhaustible—infinite—principle comes through experience of finite examples. This is the wonder of understanding. Through limited individuals, we can grasp a meaning that exceeds the limitations of those individuals: as Socrates says in the *Phaedo* (74b–d), we can grasp equality as such through experiences of particular pairs of equivalent things. Again, we can recognize a personality through a finite history of finite perspectives on a person, or something analogous through a history of experiences with our cat or dog. In these cases, the finite example functions in a way analogous to a bodily opening onto significance (such as grasping with the hand), in that it takes us beyond itself to a larger significance than it itself possesses that presents itself as the source of its own meaning. Also like those determinate bodily openings, the examples through which we proceed to insightful epiphany forever stamp our grasp of the inexhaustible form that emerges from them. Individual things offer themselves as portals to further realities, further forms, and in so doing place the stamp of their determinateness on our grasp of the infinities they make available to us. Though the forms we grasp exceed the determinate individuals through which we apprehend them, they are the very reality *of* those individuals. The realities we understand are not some determinate beings elsewhere: what we grasp are the forms that are simultaneously immanent to and transcendent of the individual things themselves.

The nature of things is, in part, to propel us toward understanding. This is not a mute or sterile dimension within experience but is, rather, an opening, a portal and a path toward another reality that is there for us if we are open to it. If we answer to the call to understand we find that there are insights available. In part, then, witnessing to the reality of things involves witnessing to *their* understandability, that is, to bear witness adequately, we must ourselves follow the path to understanding they offer. It is in the very nature of things themselves to demand of us that we work to understand them. Understanding—this grasp of the infinite forms realizing themselves within individuals—typically requires discipline, which means it requires effort and action on our part. Let us consider this "active" character of ourselves.

Our folded immersion-detachment is hard to conceive. Qua immersed, we appear passive. Qua detached, we appear active. Our own action—will—is as mysterious an epiphany as any other. And as real. We are ambiguously passive and active. It is true that the whole character of epiphany is our passivity in the face of a revelation, so it might seem that we are simply passive. There are, however, two crucial qualifications. First, the event of the epiphany is itself a reality in which we cooperate: the rhythm is only revealed to the dancing body. Second, and ultimately more far-reachingly important for these issues of developing an adequate conceptuality of ourselves, is that precisely how we find ourselves revealed to ourselves is *as active*. Indeed, we cannot claim "responsibility" for our having the powers we have, *but we do have powers*, and it would be descriptively false to portray ourselves otherwise. We are given to ourselves as beings with freedoms, power, capacities for origination, choice, and so on. Our passivity is to undergo passively the experience of being agents.

We think of our powers as "our own," and we think of our actions as "doing something to" the world. An accurate description of what happens, though, is more subtle. The power to see is just as much the visible's making itself available to us; the power to grasp is just as much the fact that the thing's own nature is such that it offers itself to our grasp. Further, every action of mine is an event that transpires in the world, that is, it is as much a happening *of* the world as it is my doing something to the world. "Our powers" are just as properly described as powers of the world. In this way, we can see that our own powers are a kind of passivity, a kind of undergoing of a given form of the world. It is equally clear, though, that we do exercise direction within the deployment of our powers; that is, one of our given powers is to be able, to some degree, to initiate and regulate the employment of these powers. As we said before, we exercise this freedom as a bird soars into the air and lands in a new location; that is, our powers are not unlimited but are the spaces for free development opened up within the determinacies of our reality.

Growth and learning are the processes of magnifying these powers and their control. Growth and learning are simultaneously heightened involvement with things and an increase in our own powers. As we move farther "out" of ourselves and become more immersed, more involved, we simultaneously "own" more—we become more powerful. Greater involvement and immersion paradoxically yield greater independence and detachment. Our growth as individuals is thus not simply a heightened separation from the world (separation from the world being the way the adult and the mind are typically construed) but is equally a deeper and deeper identification with and embeddedness in the things of our world.

It is the *practice* of engagement that produces such heightened immersion/detachment. The child learning to walk, for example, practices engaging with the household environment and gradually becomes immersed in it. This simultaneously produces a transformation of this environment from "difficult obstacles" to "supporting living room." The very determinacies of the house that were once limits to the child are now the sites of her powers: she *lives from* them rather than against them. Indeed, her life has become the veritable life *of* this environment, her actions become the realization of the possibilities of this environment: she completes the circuit whereby the needs (imperatives) of the setting are accommodated. Here we see clearly the simultaneity of increased immersion and increased detachment.

Such practice of engagement is pervasive in our formation as persons: it is the process of habituation and discipline. Habituation is the process of developing a disciplined relationship with the determinacies of a situation until one's relation with those determinacies is transformed, and one comes to grasp a deeper form that they make available. An initial grappling with the determinacies in which they are the focus of the "melodic" stream of my behavior results in a situation where those determinacies become instead the rhythmic and harmonic character and platform for a qualitatively new form of melodic action: by a history of repeated encounters, our way of living becomes fused with the parameters of a situation, and our practice becomes accustomed to *living through* these parameters. In our acquiring a habit we exchange our old limits for new: we answer to the determinacies of that which was formerly beyond ourselves. At the same time that we thus become more answerable to the nature of the situation, we equally make it our own: we "enown" a new arena.

Such enowning, such appropriation, of things is not theft. Inasmuch as our new grasp apprehends a deeper form in things, our grasp is what allows the situation to release its own deeper reality: we are its deliverance and might just as much say it has now "owned" us in that through us it is enabled to complete something about itself. Such appropriation is also not theft in that it is learning, that is, precisely what is required for such fusion is accommodation of oneself to the needs of the formerly alien determinacy. This is the case, for example, with "the convict" in William Faulkner's *The Old Man*, whose years-long teamwork with a mule has produced a deep bond between them:

> His mule (they had let him name it—John Henry) which no man save he had plowed for five years now and whose ways and habits he knew and respected and who knew his ways and habits so well that each [of] them could anticipate the other's very movements and intentions. (85)

Such habituation is not so much making things captive as it is making oneself answerable to their demands. This is the discipline of habituation: making ourselves open to determination by the other, by what *it* sets out as its needs and then living in the powers *it* affords. Enowning comes about through *work*, through engagement shaped by active respect for the demands of the other's determinacy.

Our nature is to grow by learning, and to learn by growing. In other words, we become persons through coming to know the world (in a rich sense of "know"). The epiphanies of form that populate the stages of our advances in knowledge are first and foremost the developed platforms and contexts for action and interaction that come through habituation: through effort and discipline, we are initiated into deeper involvement with the nature of things, and our growth as persons is equally the growth in the depth and complexity of the world of our experience, the world in which our "new" selves make their home.

We see here the basis for the new epistemology to accompany our new metaphysics. Knowledge is not primarily the establishment of justified, true beliefs about some alien set of affairs. It is the disciplined encounter with an alien determinacy *to overcome the alienation* and fuse with it into a new fold, a new immersion-detachment, according to which one's life is the very life of the situation; it is to live in its rhythm and to have this fusion harmonize our subsequent life affairs. Knowing is bringing to life a situation by enacting the realization of its needs. Knowing a situation *is* being its deliverance. This knowing is the very substance of our individuality, our personhood, and it is equally the substance of the world that is our home. Let us now consider this fusion, this deliverance, this knowledge, as it emerges in our experience, an experience in which learning is synonymous with growing. Wordsworth is right to say (in "My Heart Leaps Up When I Behold") that "the child is father to the man," in the sense that all adult significance develops on the basis of childhood experience. Let us, then, begin with the child.

Learning as Growth

The child grows. What the child grows into is a *world*: into a field of reality characterized by all of the structures identified in chapter 2. The experience of growth is characterized by the experience of the growing sense of "I" (among other things), and the sense of "I" is fundamentally a sense of "I can." How I experience myself is fundamentally in terms of what I am capable of, and these abilities, as we have seen, are equally the definitive powers of my "own" body and the powers afforded me by the determinate things of my world. "The self" is fundamentally a phenomenon of competence, and its attendant senses of accomplishment and aspiration (and its essential contextualizing, as we shall see, by incompetency), all of which are articulated in the terms of the things of the world.

The growing significance of the "I can" that derives from the child's "own body" is matched by a growing richness to things—the common fabric they weave grows more complex and systematic, and the individual things themselves develop greater consistency—and a growing integration with other people, who themselves take on more clearly defined personalities. Reality simultaneously becomes more deeply differentiated and more tightly interwoven, denser and more articulate, rhythmically and harmonically more rich and melodically more intricate. This growth, and the burgeoning world it clears, is itself an epiphany: the child witnesses this growing, polytemporal complexity without, strictly speaking, *doing* it or being able to stop it, and yet it is the child itself who is growing in this growth, and it is precisely a growth in personal agency that is the most obvious fruit of this development. For our description here, we have distinguished between "body," "things," "self," and "others," but these very distinctions are a development of the dynamism of reality, not its source. It is with the child's development that we can perhaps most clearly grasp this, for we can see in the child that initial nonisolation of these elements.

The child is born into a world not of its own making. For the adult onlooker, the situation can be described according to all the familiar categories of developed experience: we say that this small human baby is in a house using its arms and legs to crawl to its mother. For the child, however, the situation is quite different. The child's experience is not yet organized according to these categories, and it will precisely be the achievement of its growth to come to experience the world as the adult does. Julia Kristeva, in her work *Revolution in Poetic Language*, describes this original bodily state of the child-in-situation as the "semiotic *chora*":

> Discrete quantities of energy move through the body of the subject who is not yet constituted as such and, in the course of his development, they are arranged according to the various constraints imposed on this body . . . by family and social structures. [This is] an essentially mobile and extremely provisional articulation constituted by movements and their ephemeral states. . . . We differentiate this uncertain and indeterminate *articulation* from a *disposition* that already depends on representation . . . . Neither model nor copy, the *chora* precedes and underlies figuration and thus specularization, and is analogous only to vocal or kinetic rhythm. (25–26, emphases in original)

For the child, experience is the wealth of wondrous contacts, the wealth of significance pouring into it from so many novel angles. What the adult calls "a hand grabbing an object" is for the child a happening of significance, determinately shaped by the forms of its embodiment but not yet known in those terms. The child's body—hands, mouth, anus, windpipe, skin—is so many determinate routes for meaning—routes for a meaning always figured by the specificities of those bodily powers that are lived through being enhanded, enmouthed, and so on. The child's experience happens at the point of contact of the determinate potential that is its immediate embodiment and the determinate potential that is its surrounding environment. It is this contact itself that is the world—the experience—of the child. This contact is not a matter of a mind "thinking thoughts," not a "representation" of its situation but an *inhabiting* of it, a coupling or "pairing" of body and world. This implies three things.

That the child's experience is established as a contact, a coupling, of body of world, implies, first, that meaning for the child is always and originally figured by the forms of significance made available to it by the specifics of its embodiment: all meaning is originally rooted in the schemata for possible meaning that emanate from the powers and sensitivities of our bodies. It implies, second, that meaning is always rooted in the already established determinacies of the material, historical determinacies of its environment as those things make themselves available to our bodily sensibilities. It implies, third, that, inasmuch as the child is not approaching the world from an already established alien domain (an onlooking, representational mind), the very norms with which the child operates in dealing with this realm of contact must themselves emerge within this contact; said otherwise, the child's original situation of "knowing" is equally a situation of "playing," in that it is not answering—indeed, in principle is not answerable

to—any norm beyond this situation, except insofar as that "beyond" imma-
nently emerges from within the situation itself. In all these senses, then, we
can see that it is *within* the domain and parameters of meaning opened up
in this contact that subsequent experience emerges.

The history of the child's development is the history of its becoming
familiar with these significances, its learning to navigate and use this
world of contact. Through this dynamic contact the child gradually becomes habituated to systems of "making sense" in a progressively developing fashion; this habituation is the process of something like a "lived
induction," whereby we move from an acquaintance with a finite set of
specific experiences to an experience of a general sense of an entire
realm of meaning. In walking, for example, a child initially struggles to
control the relation between its limbs and the surrounding environment
of earth and air. Through a history of specific struggles, the child enters
into a *qualitatively new form* of bodily-spatial relationship. Learning to walk
through a *particular* and finite set of interactions transforms the character of limb-earth relation from "alienating" to "comfortable" and furthermore makes this whole struggle a *settled* conflict, the successful
resolution of which is now the acquisition of a permanent or *universal*
structure upon which newer, more sophisticated experiences of action
will be built. Through habituation—familiarization with characteristic
modes of successful contact—we develop the reliable base of involvement from which we can move on to engagements with grander forms of
significance. The habit supplies the secure rhythmic platform upon
which and the stable harmonic character within which we make contact
with new, more advanced realities.

This ability to advance to greater and greater levels of sophistication
in the forms of determinacy that can be meaningful to us is the miracle
of our embodiment. It is the dual character of the body simultaneously
to let us into the world of determinate significance while imparting its
specific form to this whole realm of determinacy. The determinacy that
is our body is simultaneously the power to be in the world and the limi-
tation to the form in which we can be in the world. Learning—getting to
know the world—is precisely becoming empowered to navigate in the
world, which means becoming familiar with the ways in which the world
affords us opportunities for sense. The sense we make of our world, however, is permanently figured by the determinate routes our singular
embodiment offers us for making contact.

Perhaps the most important sphere of sense that we must come to
navigate as we grow is the sense of "humanity" that pervades our world.
Our world is a world of human persons, and it is this sense of learning,
aspiring, creative, communicative beings that we must contact if we are
to come to recognize ourselves as persons and, necessarily correlatively,

our environment as a human environment shaped by other persons. Let us look at the child's development of the sense of "other persons" in particular.

Humanity and Tragedy

Like all sense, the sense of the human is a sense with which we engage through the forms of meaning opened to us through our bodies and through the processes of habituation and familiarization by which we come to have a sense of a stable environment in which we can proceed on our projects of making sense. The sense "other person," or just "person," emerges for us on the basis of the history of our habituation to this sense as it develops through our self-transcending bodily engagement with a finite set of actual contacts with specific individuals. Just as the determinacies of our body permanently shape our sense of the human, so do the determinacies of contact through which we historically came to develop our familiarity with others shape this sense. In our discussion of insight, we saw that our identities as perceivers naturally develop into identities as knowers. As we now investigate the essential relation between our families and our lived familiarities with the human world, we will see that our identities as perceivers also develop into identities as family members, and that it is only within this context that we further develop our identities as individuals.

"The family" is, primarily, those others through whom—or with whom—the single human being becomes habituated to the sense "person." Our families are those people who were historically exemplary for affording us the opportunity to contact the sense "human world." As Simone de Beauvoir notes in chapter 2 of *The Ethics of Ambiguity*, parents are for the child like gods, the originative and controlling sources of all meaning. As children, we experience the world *as* the site for engaging *with them*, just as they are our routes into engaging with the world: reality for the child is a fused sense of world/parents, and there is no success with respect to either side of that sense without success with respect to the other side. This is the experiential reality of "the family." It is an *interhuman* world into which the child is growing up, and successfully engaging with that sense ("the interhuman world") entails successfully learning to navigate those parts of the child's reality that are parents, siblings, or other core family members: inhabiting the world *as human* comes through learning how to "couple" successfully with those other people who, through their already established powers that far exceed those of the child, in fact hold the position of offering to the child the routes of entry into meaning. The other humans who surround the child, through their physical and educational power, have the primary capacity to engage the child's bodily capacities for sensing. Whether we are orphans or children born into "normal" family life, we must necessarily have such a family in that it will always be through a history of specific interactions with specific others that we become habituated to the sense "our world," the "human world," the sense in the context of which we derive or develop our own self-designation as "person." The family, that is, is a historical, determinate structure that functions within the experience of anyone who says "I"—the experience therefore of any person—and it is the structure by which that person has come to develop a habitual familiarity with the sense "human."

This is the basis of the ambiguity of interpersonal life, of the inherently tragic character of our existence. Our sense of our own identity as "human" is rooted in a history of habituation, and, like all habituation, it bears the marks of that finitude that is its condition, namely, the finitude of bodily form, and the finitude of the specific contacts through which we became habituated. It is the inescapably particular character of our familial familiarity with the human that leaves our sense of our own identity always tragically defined by a disparity between our concept of ourselves—what we think we should be—and our actuality—what our singular situation allows us to realize. In the language of the body, our reach, with respect to our sense of ourselves, always tragically exceeds our grasp. Let us see how this is so.

Our sense of our human identity is a sense we carry with us in our bodily grasp of our world. It is a sense gleaned by what was impressed upon us by those specific others through whom we became accustomed to intersubjective life. The family is those specific others who happened to form the intersubjective environment in which we grew into the possession of an adult personality, and its formative and continuing meaning for our self-identity is the specific history of inauguration into the significance of intersubjective life that we carry within our developed bodily comportment toward the world. Its continuing significance is as that concentrated memory of intersubjective history that forms, for the adult person, the determinate *form* of significance that pervades the experience of the world *as a human world*, and that is a pervasive platform and character of sense that is contacted through all of our behavior. The legacy of the family is found in *how* the human world is sensed *as human* through all of our bodily sensitivities.

The specific dynamics of the process of contacting the sense of "self and others"—that is, the process by which the sense of oneself as a person is developed through interaction with others—is a process of struggling for power and recognition, a process of learning to navigate the vulnerability we have to the perspective of others upon us in determining how, or even whether, we matter to them. Let us see why.

As self-aware subjects, we experience ourselves as centers of meaning and importance (we experience ourselves in the first person, as a subject for ourselves), and yet, as we saw in chapter 2, we also experience ourselves as placed in a world of other subjects that would get along just fine without us (we experience ourselves in the third person, as an object for others). The process of dealing with other people is fundamentally shaped by our struggle to resolve this tension between our sense of ourselves as the most important thing—the center of all of our experience—and our sense of ourselves as completely insignificant, the tension of the ambiguous "here" and "there" of our bodily *ecstasis* that we encountered earlier. On our own, we cannot settle this issue, because it is only the other who can show, through his or her words or behavior, whether I do in fact matter to him or her. In dealing with others, it is this answer to this question that we look for—just as they look for that answer from us—and it is how these delicate and complex matters of mutual evaluation are handled that will determine how we end up being able to frame and live with a basic sense of ourselves as persons.

The very notion of "I"—the notion of our most personal, most singular reality—is thus a communally or cooperatively established notion. Who I am is something that, alone, I can only propose as a hypothesis, subject to coordination with your interpretation of who I am. To find myself, I must seek your perspective upon me, and that means my most intimate sense of myself is inherently vulnerable to the power of your judgment. For each of us, our "outside" is very much a part of our identity, but this outside, this part of ourselves, is not in our own control: how we appear to others is something that is judged *by them.* Only others can tell me whether I am kind or cruel, interesting or boring, friendly or cold, "cool" or "a jerk." These designations specify *what kind of person I am* at the very core, and the judgment of others is thus placed at the most significant location in our lives. The assessment of others is essential to us, and we feel this vulnerability in the deep hurt or deep pleasure we undergo when we encounter these assessments.

Though one can imagine a dialogue of harmonious mutuality happening between us, in which we both are insightful, fair, kind, candid, and responsive in our estimations of each other and in the communication of this through our behavior, it is nonetheless typically the case that in our dealings with each other we are antagonistic, competitive, defensive, mean, timid, ignorant, or dishonest. We feel our vulnerability to others, and we often respond to this in unhealthy ways: we respond aggressively by trying to intimidate the other person so as to "get the upper hand" in this power struggle; we respond submissively, accepting in advance the other's superiority in order not to risk disappointment; we act in denial by attempting to adopt an attitude of cold indifference to the other and her judgment; or we act manipulatively, trying to construct a seductive or threatening or nonthreatening image of ourselves through which to gain access to the other's will while shielding ourselves from his gaze. Virginia Woolf's *The Waves* displays powerfully these ways in which we live out our personalities in terms of such dynamic struggles of interpersonal struggle and recognition. In her portraits of Neville, forever defining himself by his desire for Percival's affection (e.g., pp. 36–37), of Louis, constantly grappling with his discomfort at how he imagines his social status to appear in the eyes of others (e.g., pp. 14, 19), or of Jinny, who builds her life around the support of adoring others (e.g., pp. 43, 49), for example, Woolf demonstrates very effectively how a personality is shaped is terms of this interplay of mutual recognition, and how the positions one adopts in these interactions have a continuing impact throughout the course of one's life. We are ongoingly wrapped up in these strategies in our regular dealings with our companions, and, more importantly, it was through such dealings with our family members that our basic sense of ourselves as persons was formed.

In navigating with the sense of the human, with the sense of ourselves as persons, it is this sense of our place in the dialectic of desire, power, and recognition that we contact, and in the involvement with the world into which our family initiates us, it is our position in this struggle to which we are fundamentally becoming habituated. When we engage with this dialogue of mutual assessment in our childhood dealings with our parents, siblings, grandparents, and so on, we are not dealing with an optional human context in which we as individuals can enter or from which we as individuals can withdraw at will; on the contrary, this familial context is our home—it is where we *are*, most fundamentally—and is therefore not optional but necessary. The intersubjective context of family life, in other words, is the very medium within which I live as "I," and it is in the internal dynamics of *this* interpersonal "here" that my sense of who I am—my sense of what it is to be an "I"—is learned. The family reality is the sense of the human that informs our adult experience, and that means that our familial identity is the way we remember our role in our founding experience of the dialectic of recognition.

In our behavior, we ongoingly remember the family—we remember ourselves—as the way that we experience our place in the dialectic of recognition and, specifically, experience it *as* the rhythm and harmony of all of our bodily behavior—in our abilities to walk, to grasp, to eat, to speak—and *as* the texture of the things we grasp, eat, and so on: in walking through the yard, sitting on the couch, drinking milk, and talking about the weather, I grapple with the family reality through which my own identity was formed, for my initial engagement with these practices was *as* constitutive aspects of my engagement with my familial world, and the very texture of their meaning is the way they hold me in the pattern of the interplay of mutual recognition that was performed in my familial initiation into these realities. We continue to live our family membership as the way that our bodily engagement with the world is shaped by the demands of answering to the power struggles of intersubjective life. Much of our familial initiation into human life will be successful and will usher us into an independent adulthood of competent engagement with the world. But since the power struggles of intersubjective life do not typically lead to a fully healthy and wholesome fulfillment of our intersubjective pursuit of self-esteem, we also typically live our ongoing family identity in large or small part as the reminders of how our humanity has been crippled through the mishandling of our vulnerabilities by our familiar others. One of the most compelling and beautiful portrayals of this dimension of human life is Faulkner's *The Sound and the Fury*, perhaps most strikingly in its portrait of Jason, whose whole character seems perpetually to enact a resentful striking back at his upbringing, and this is all he can see *in* every thing in the world, *in* every practice. In other words, in one's adult life, the family has a continuing existence in one's intersubjective competencies and in one's hang-ups, one's incompetencies. Perhaps as an adult I cannot get over a basic "eagerness to please" that was formed in my childhood and that now manifests itself in my conversational style, my dressing style, my approach to my job; perhaps a sense of my own weakness and inadequacy to the task was impressed upon me so deeply as a child that my adult commitment to unrelenting hard work is coupled with a constant depression or sense of disappointment. Our competencies and our incompetencies are interwoven, and they are interwoven in ways that we are not immediately free to change. As the essential matrix of our formation as independent individuals, the family lingers within us as the ways we are unable fully to assume the stance of independence and individuality. In this way, the family repeats the basic character of the body.

Our bodies open us to meaning—their very character is to be transcending themselves toward . . . . It is to our bodies that we owe everything. Nonetheless, there is something right about the sense of the body as a prison for the soul. The body is that from which we can never get away; this is particularly true in the way that the form and the history of our embodiment are carried forward in all of our ways of making sense. We all have humble origins—our hands, our mouth, our anus—and our greatest, most sophisticated involvements all betray these roots. This, as we have seen, is the double structure of the body: to propel us beyond our immediate situation into the world of generalities, comprehensions, principles, and laws—the realm, in short, of universality—while simultaneously holding us within a particularity. It is through our embodiment that we are given access to community, to reason, to science, to law, yet we always enter into these realms from a perspective. Our bodies lead us into this world of meanings that seem to demand that we shed our biases, our particularities, yet it is only by living out of a particular bias that we have access to this world. This double structure of embodiment makes for a double structure to our experience. We are always drawn compellingly both by the inherent demands of the universal and the necessary and by the lived demands of the particular and the contingent. Our experience cannot help being shaped by these two directions within experience, which themselves conflict with each other.

This same tension is present in the family. The very nature of the family is to inaugurate us into the world of persons, the world in which each individual assumes the identity of an autonomous adult. Our initiation into the human world beyond the family is realized as our experience of ourselves as single, autonomous individuals, constrained by values that are indifferent to our local specificities, answerable to the universal and necessary demands that accrue to us all as formally discrete selves. Yet the very route into this meaning of "humanity" or "person as such" cannot be stripped, for us, of its familial origins, of its specificities and its rootedness. The task of the family is to send us clear of the family, into the larger social world of free individuals; yet the very nature of the family is always to keep its own character as the root of our sense of the human. We are always, as Freud suggests, dealing with mother figures and father figures. The tragedy of family life is that it is that by which we escape our familial childhood, while simultaneously being that from which we can never escape. The tragedy and wonder of embodiment is that it always throws us beyond ourselves, making us open to ever-greater sense while always holding us down to a determinacy we can never shake. In the form of the family, the tragedy is the way we are let into the world of free, self-conscious humanity without ever being able to enter that realm fully. Our tragedy is that we cannot be cured of our family legacy.

The family, then, is a form inherent to human experience. It is our entry into intersubjectivity; it is the foundation of our experience of familiarity; it is a memory of power relations; and, ultimately, it is the path by which we assume our identity as individuals, but always imperfectly. The family makes a unique contribution to human experience in that it is the phenomenon of the initiation into familiarity with others. This familiarity is a *conditio sine qua non* of any human experience qua human, and it is thus the ground of all other social forms while being reducible to none. It has the responsibility for inaugurating our social existence and is therefore situated at the most vulnerable point in our identity. It is to the family that we owe our entry into the experiences of dignity, intimacy, and uniqueness that mark our existence as persons, but it is also to the family that we owe the fact that these experiences are typically scarred or crippled in repressive ways.

We, as single selves, are always simultaneously local and global, determinate and universal. Our own identity is thus ambiguously to be perceiver and knower, to be family member and individual. Epistemically, we will always be torn between the perceptual demands of the thing in its absoluteness and the conceptual demands of the relatedness and groundedness of things. Politically, we will always be bound by the conflicting values of a particular family and universal society. This is the tragic character of our embodiment.

Humanity and Learning

It is the very nature of our familial identity to open us onto a reality beyond the family and an identity beyond family membership. That human reality beyond is the world in which one is an individual, a representative, equal in principle to every other, of humanity in general. Entering as such an individual into the sphere of adult human relations is a process (which will be a central theme in chapter 4): it is something that must be accomplished, something done in cooperation with others, and something transformative—indeed, it is a creative process in which the person we are to become is brought into being. Our participation as free, individual persons in "humanity" as such is not something given but is something that must be accomplished by each of us: we must *learn how* to be a free individual.

Learning to be a free individual is equally learning about others, for it is a matter of learning what it is to be an equal representative of humanity, that is, it is a learning of the universal character of humanity. This learning, furthermore, has two different dimensions. On the one hand, this learning is a practical matter, a question of developing the practice of behaving as a free individual in a human society. On the other hand, this learning is a theoretical matter, a question of explicitly coming to understand oneself and persons in general as free individuals. In both aspects of this learning we can be more or less successful, and these two forms of "knowing"—the behavioral and the explicitly self-reflective—can be at odds with each other. Let us consider both this behavioral process of learning to be an individual person—a free and an equal participant in universal humanity—and our insight (or lack thereof) into our nature as persons.

In family life, we are initiated into a primal intimacy, an originary sharing of identity that prefigures our sharing of humanity as such (prefigures in the sense that it anticipates and propels us toward a superfamilial reality, and in the sense that it figures in advance the character of that experience). We are *initiates* into humanity: it is a reality we must learn. To say that we must "learn" it is to stress that humanity is a reality that is not something simply given to us but something accessible only through the effort of accommodating ourselves to its nature and identifying with it. But human reality also is not simply given in the sense that it is a reality that does not preexist its performance by humans: it is a reality in which we must participate, so in part it also is a reality that we must make. The sense of "creative participation" will be our topic in chapter 4. Let us first consider more closely the sense of "learning" that is involved in our assuming of our humanity.

Our humanity is achieved only as learning, and learning is, as we have seen, coming to identify with the other, coming to share its reality. As we shall see in chapter 4, our learning of others is interwoven with our learning of things: to share, to develop our humanity, is to put ourselves into *the world, communally.* Our embrace of our humanity is not a separate set of acts from our learning of the world. For the moment, though, let us focus on this process of learning from the side of the experience we have in it of other persons. In particular, let us look again at the experience of the child and see how it opens up onto the experience of learning, through others, the character of a reality and an identity beyond family life. Let us first think about the nature of the child's upbringing and the way in which it is simultaneously a specific way of behaviorally learning to be someone and a specific way of learning to think of oneself and one's identity, and then consider the experience of others within that context.

As we saw earlier, it is through the child's upbringing that the child is inaugurated into the experience of being someone. Like all inaugural experiences, this inauguration into intersubjective life leaves the stamp of its specific character on the broader experiences that develop out of it. Our adult perspective on a child's upbringing allows us to recognize the idiosyncrasy and contingency of the specific forms that upbringing takes. This is because as adults we see this upbringing as a set of particular human interactions able to be compared to many others of which we have had experience or that we can imagine, and because we can think about the grounds, causes, and principles involved throughout these interactions. For the child, however, its upbringing is not one set of optional behaviors comparable to others and situated within an established world of grounds and principles but is, on the contrary, the unique and nonoptional route through which those very experiences of comparison and situating become possible. By looking, as adults, to our principled insight into "the way things are," we can evaluate the relative significance of the contingent specificity of this particular process of upbringing. For the child, however, this process *is* the way things are: *it* is normative for all else, rather than being contextualized by some more fundamental norm. Though our perception of another's family life affords us the critical distance necessary to judge it by the standards of the world, our experience of our own familial reality is the experience of something that "just is the way it is": though our familial experience *is* in fact something that is performatively accomplished, for the child (and therefore for all of us, at root) it is *experienced* as something simply *given*. In our family life we begin to learn to be persons, but the character of "being someone" that we learn is something we learn *as* something simply given.

Our familial experience also, however, opens us up to the world of people beyond the family who exemplify for us the human possibilities beyond what is given in the family, and this dimension of our experience has important consequences for our "education" into our humanity. The other people in our familial world—members of other families or lone individuals from beyond the horizons of our family world—are experienced by us both as familiar and as strange, as both already the same as us and as alien beings. They are familiar in that we take them to be versions of the same reality that we presume to be "given," but they are strange in that they do not conform to the ways "we" (in our family) actually do things. We do not initially treat our humanity as something we need to learn: we are secure in our familial sense—the harmony of our everyday life—that we know how things are, and we treat others as being in the wrong insofar as they differ from us and our presumptions regarding legitimate (and necessary) behavior. But though our initial familial reflex is to denigrate the distinctive nature of these strange others, these strangers nonetheless also offer us a pathway to seeing things otherwise. With education and the self-transformations of personal development that accompany our progressive entry in a postfamilial society of independent individuals, we can come to recognize the alienness of other people as evidence of legitimate possibilities of a free life rather than as evidence of their insufficiency: what we initially experience as the strangeness of the other is ultimately an experience of the openness of our own future, of our possibilities to be otherwise. In this way, we experience our humanity as something to be *achieved*, something yet to come. Accomplishing this learning requires a fundamental change in the "harmonic" structure of our life, that is, in the very sense of the *meaning* of our interpersonal actions that are the melodies of our human world.

We learn who we are—who we can be—through our experience of others. Initially, through our establishing a sense of their familiarity, we develop a comfortable sense of who we are, a sense we treat as if it were simply given. Ultimately, though, the experience of the strangeness of others affords us the experience of our own potential to be otherwise, which is the recognition of our freedom, the recognition that our humanity must be accomplished. It requires time and learning to overcome the dogmatism of our familial presumptions, to learn that our own nature—our freedom—calls upon us to take responsibility for ourselves in shaping how we will be human, and it is not guaranteed that we will come to recognize this characteristic of our own nature. Typically, in contemporary Western culture, we do make this transition, and we do come to construe ourselves as free individuals—the "rights-bearing" individuals of democratic society, the individuals characterized by the "universal human rights" for which Malcolm X, for example, so valiantly struggled. What we are seeing is that this learning to live as a free and an equal individual is something *accomplished*, but our learning to understand ourselves as free individuals does not automatically acknowledge this character of "accomplishment."

Typically, we as (Western) adults experience ourselves unproblematically as "humans." What we typically take to be this "humanity" is really the *achieved* adulthood into which we grow from our familial beginnings, but even as we think of ourselves *as* free individuals, rather than *as* family members, we typically assume about ourselves that we are *automatically* such autonomous, "rights-bearing" individuals. This way of existing as a person is not, however, something that automatically obtains in reality. As we have seen, this situation of responsible adulthood (1) has a history, in the dynamics of family life, and (2) is a shared social achievement rather than something one automatically possesses on one's own. In our everyday perception of our own humanity we typically misconstrue our own nature, mistaking our achieved, communal identity for an independent reality that is simply and nonhistorically given. We confuse the stance of the adult in society with human "nature." Even though we have gone through a process of "learning" to be human, we typically do not notice this about ourselves, and, like the child, we accept our accomplished nature as something simply given. Even as we grow beyond our familial identity, something like our familial dogmatism continues in our presumption of our "given" humanity.

The result of these misconstruals that characterize our living perception is that we typically have adopted inadequate concepts for thinking about our reality, not just in our daily affairs but in our most advanced conceptual endeavors. These mistaken presumptions about human nature are at the foundation of much philosophy, much political theory, much social and legal policy, and much psychological practice. We have noted already the inadequacy of the reductive concepts of physics, chemisty, and biology to comprehend the human world, and this is equally true of approaches in the explicitly human studies that operate with a concept of the person as a given, fully formed, autonomous individual. In fact, the person achieves whatever autonomy and individuality she achieves only on the basis of *developing* the *given* powers of her immersed-detached *embeddedness* in a thingly, interhuman, and linguistic world. Our humanity is realized only in a developmental process and only through the support of others, and for that reason humanity cannot be adequately comprehended without concepts such as "maturity" (a concept taken from biology, which applies only ambiguously to the person inasmuch as human nature does not have an unambiguous "completion"), "sharing," and more.

Also inadequate in principle are philosophies or theories, which typically accompany the atomistic approaches to the human that we have just criticized—that cannot theoretically accommodate our experience of other people as such. According to the methods of natural science and the presumptions of much social science, it is an irresolvable puzzle how we could ever encounter another person: the familiar theories of how we acquire knowledge base their theories on the presumption that knowledge is "information," and that learning happens through the mechanical impress of sensory data on sensory organs, but such methods will never explain the epiphany of another person (nor, indeed, the experience of any inexhaustible "infinite," any experience of a beyond that exceeds the finite determinacies of the history of our experience). And yet we *do* experience others. An adequate philosophy must *start* from the recognition of this fact. Any philosophy that finds the experience of other persons logically or methodologically impossible is, ipso facto, an inadequate philosophy of the person.

We recognize other *people*. Reality for us is the human world. Our talk earlier of "mystery," "revelation," and "epiphany," and of "rhythm," "tragedy," and "immersion," may have suggested a reality different from our own, a reality of sorcerers and fairy tales, but in fact the reality comprehended by these concepts is precisely our day-to-day world of life with other people. This language is necessary, however, to emphasize the distance between the form our experience actually takes and the conceptual approaches we usually bring to our interpretation of this experience. Whether in our familial dogmatism, in which we presume that our human reality is naturally given in the form it happens to take in our family life, or in our theoretical studies, in which we take our accomplished adult individuality as the whole form of our human reality, we see that, though it is ultimately our nature to be called to witness to our own character as witnesses (as we shall discover), it is not the case that we automatically construe ourselves or others aright. We have seen that we do in fact experience other people, and that the form this experience takes does not fit into the pattern of many of our familiar conceptual approaches. Just as our humanity must itself be learned, so must we learn an adequate conceptuality. Specifically, we must learn to take up our human reality, both behaviorally and conceptually, as something essentially shared and essentially ambiguous in the ways we have so far been identifying.

Humanity and Art

Our reality is fundamentally enacted in our participation in a world with other people. Our reality is human. This reality is not one we are born with, and not one we possess on our own. We discover our human nature, we enact it, and we create it only in our engagement with others. In our family life, we are initiated into our humanity, but the family is not the realm of human fulfillment. The family is itself a self-transcending reality that throws us outside itself into the human world as such.

Humanity is a reality, but not a reality realizable by any single body. This is the essential nature of the human: sharing. Sharing is the epiphanic reality that is our humanity. We have seen already that reality as such is characterized by the reciprocal immersion of things with each other, with people, and so on. Such immersion does not just "characterize" us, however: we *live* this immersion. This is sharing: to *experience* the "with" and the "in." The very nature of sharing, of course, is such that it can be revealed only in being shared, that is, it can never be revealed as a strictly alien object but can only be revealed in being performed. Humanity is the performance of being human, the effecting of sharing. Humanity as the performance of sharing can only be realized intercorporeally, can only be done *together*. Humanity rests on our immersion in each other; it is realized through communication.

We must *live* our immersion in another to *share*: we must *experience* being *with*. This is the accomplishment of communication. When we communicate, we bring into being a world that exists for us *as* a couple or *as* a community. Through your words or your gestures, I am transported into a world, into a way of living or seeing: your words are not the *object* of my experience but are the medium by which I am able to witness the reality you invoke. And that world invoked by you is already a perspective, a way of being of the world in relation to you. Your expression communicates your witnessing, and in my participation in this communication I am witness to your witnessing in my very experience of witnessing the world you invoke. The successful communication is our act of co-witnessing, our sharing of an activity of witnessing.

When we communicate we bring our witnessing to explicitude and allow another to be witness to it. Communication is bringing our witnessing to expression. It is only with communication that our humanity is accomplished, that we actually share. In other words, it is expression—art—that allows us to be human, that allows us to share, for art is the bringing to expression of our witnessing. Art facilitates humanity by offering to each an epiphany of reality as such, a witnessing to the very nature of witnessing. In sharing this vision, we witness together. All forms of distinctively human experience will thus be rooted in artistic expression.

The primal intimacy of family life is rooted in such expressive co-witnessing. Children build their engagement with reality through the gestures of their parents (or parental surrogates) and develop a system of *being-with*, develop a capacity for sharing, by taking on those gestures as true, effective, and reliable: children become articulate by undergoing a kind of "artistic revolution" and allowing their reality to be articulated by the gestures of the surrounding family. Learning the language is accepting the revelatory powers of these gestures, that is, it is giving oneself over to their rhythm, trusting in their power to realize the real. Learning the language is, like dancing, allowing one's body—one's own gestural powers— to be taken over and directed by the *given* forms.

Learning the language—accepting the revelatory powers of these gestures—and contacting the perspective of the others are one and the same activity, one and the same reality: in learning the language, the child is living within the perspective—living within the world—of the others. Children grow into the world by learning a "language," in the sense of nouns, syntax, and so on, but also by learning the language of bodily gesture, the language of toilet practices, the language of dressing style, and the language of household comportment. *All* of the materials of the world are sites for communication, gestural media for co-witnessing, media for communicating what it is to be human. For witnesses to epiphany— humans—the real is the reality of gesture. The child learns how to (behaviorally) read and write in all things "co-participation in reality."

The original togetherness, the primal intimacy, established through family life is thus the development of a commitment to a system of gesture, a system of expression. It is *by recognizing the meaning of the situation thus*, recognizing the world as its family demands it be recognized, that the child shares, that the child enters the human world offered by the family. To enter the family is to be committed to a "take" on reality, to be committed to a way of finding reality expressive/expressed.

For this reason, family life is thus inherently "religious," in that to participate in the family reality is to accept a set of expressive gestures— rituals, images—as privileged, essential revelations of truth. There is, to be sure, more to the phenomenon of religion than this point alone, but it is characteristically religious to insist on the necessity and truth of images, stories, rituals, and artifacts that members of another (equally religious) culture consider contingent, and this worship/idolatry is the nature of the child's familial experience. Though the system of gesture into which the child grows bears the marks of the idiosyncrasy and contingency of the practices of *this* family and *this* culture, to the child it is not one option among many but *the* way to the real, *the* way to co-witnessing. Thus what we earlier called the tragedy of family life also can be called the inherent religiosity of human life: family life initiates us into co-witnessing by an "expressive dogmatism," by inducing in the child a sense of the unique necessity of the system of gesture into which it is born.

The artistic foundation of our humanity thus originally gives rise to a religious form of co-witnessing, a familial piety, as it were. At the same time, by transporting us into the human world, it offers us the epiphany of the human as such, of the possibility of a world beyond the family—a world in which we are already implicated in principle, in which we are already called to participate by our very nature. This participation, however, can only be realized through the openness of dialogue, through *forging* links with others, and this by terms that exceed those of our family piety. The inherent exigency of our nature—the demand our humanity makes upon us to fulfill it beyond the realm of the family—thus propels us beyond art-as-religion to art-as-dialogue, that is, to expression as an explicitly creative redefinition of the parameters of our co-witnessing.

Imperatives

The growth of the child is *learning*. We have considered this in general in our consideration of the growing immersion in the world that comes with habituation, and we have considered it in the specific domain of our "knowledge" of our own humanity; we have seen that this learning is inseparable from the embrace of a language. Learning is perhaps what is most amazing in this whole epiphanic world: the phenomenon of advance in insight. Earlier we spoke of the perceptual field and its propulsion toward understanding/being understood. This propulsion is the very life of the child: the child hears reality as the rhythm of learning. Here (to speak in terms of the dualistic language that treats subject and object as separate, which, we have seen, is a part truth) we can see both the character of the person (child) *to understand, to learn,* and the character of things *to be understood, to be learned.* It is our nature to grow in insight and comprehension and appreciation and ability, and it is the nature of the situation to call for this growth and to afford and enable its possibility. Let us look further at the "worldly" side of this learning.

Our situation propels us forward. *It* propels us to act, to learn, to speak. It is the ambiguous nature of things that is the condition of learning: only a being who can experience the ambiguity in reality can learn. Though the ambiguities that characterize reality will never be "settled," they nonetheless drive us constantly to resolve their tensions. The very nature of things throws us toward resolution and universality. In fact, the actual resolutions that we go on to accomplish and the tensions to which they answer are always specific, though they rest upon the fundamental tensions that characterize the very nature of our reality in principle, that is, though our situation as a whole is always thrown toward universality and resolution, that situation itself is nonetheless always specific, determinate, and this specificity is always experienced by us as so many specific pressures, so many determinate calls toward couplings, separatings, interventions, detachments, and so on. At the melodic level of ongoing affairs, this tap needs to be shut off, this hunger needs to be satiated, this letter needs to be answered, this silence needs to be preserved, this problem in our conversation needs to be understood and resolved. At a deeper level of harmonic resonance and rhythmic flow, the emerging morning calls me to begin my day, the presence of my mother calls me to be deferential and to live with a feeling of self-loathing, our being in our house together calls us to relax in our companionship and to embark on the activities we enjoy. The propulsion toward resolution is pervasive, but it is experienced through the call toward particular imperatives. The specificities, the local identities, of the metaphysically magnetic things that we perceive are, like the music, always calls to constructive response, powers that are realized only by setting up a charge in our bodies. Our new metaphysics, then, must also recognize that the call, the "should," the imperative itself is inherent to the very nature of phenomenal reality and that its presentation is multiple: reality is the epiphany of so many "oughts."

These "oughts" are a helpful route to understanding our single nature as the immersed-detached fold. The "oughts" reveal our immersion in that the intrinsic needs of things are lived as our ownmost experience. They reveal our detachment in that the very character of the "ought" is such as not to be capable of guaranteeing its own realization "on its own." In other words, our detachment is the necessity that we "on our own" *act* to accomplish this necessity. We can be the "deliverance" of things only by both being and not-being them: being them, so as to enact *their* needs, not-being them, so as to *enact* their needs.

This notion of learning, growing, and answering to the needs of the situation allows us to see more clearly the nature of our status as witnesses. To witness is not simply to look on; it is not simply to be a recorder of a fact or an event. In ancient Greek, the word for witness is "*martyr.*" The Christian "martyrs" were "witnesses to the faith," that is, they were devoted (to the point of death) to the recognition of the revealed truth. "Witnessing" did not mean merely noting that something had happened; "witnessing" meant orienting one's life around the need to answer to the epiphany, the miraculous revelation of a truth that has *claimed* one's ownmost essence. It is in a like sense that we are witnesses to epiphany. We are claimed by our situation: we are called, and only our commitment will answer the call, will deliver the situation. As in the familiar navigation of daily discourse, so in our ownmost nature is our role to be the link that completes a circuit and allows a current to flow. Our essence is to be witnesses to epiphany in that it is only through our action, our commitment, that the animating tensions of our world can win their resolution.

It is *as witnesses* that we are growing, which means that growing up into ourselves—which is equally growing up into the world—is growing up into commitment.

In our growth, then, we become, as we have seen, simultaneously more immersed and more detached. As we grow, so too does our world grow. With our growing immersion-detachment, the world with which we are involved itself becomes both more differentiated and more integrated; along with this, too, its character takes on a progressively stronger character of imperative, of a call to commitment that corresponds to our own stronger experience of detachment. Our growing relationship with the world thus expands simultaneously along three axes: we become simultaneously more involved, more independent, and more called to greater commitment.

Our commitment is always and will always be specific. Though we can adopt the stance of science and duty and orient ourselves by the universal, it will always be particular actions in particular situations that we will undertake. Our actions will always have a time and a place, a particular community, and so on. It will always be *this* person who solicits my care, *this* budget that needs to be balanced, *this* soil that needs to be tilled. There is indeed an epiphany of the universal—we are called to truth and duty—but our aspirations in this direction can only ever be realized through engagement with our surroundings. The universal is not reached by turning elsewhere but can only be a call to engage (all the more fervently) with *these things*.

We can never avoid commitment. To act—to live—will always be to respond to various calls that emerge for us from within our own situation. And yet there is a distinction within these commitments. It is the nature of our habitual commitments to call us to carry out the dancing to habitual rhythms that is the ongoing flow of our established lives; but beyond this calling, it also is the very nature of our setting—the setting of things and other persons—to call us *to commitment as such*. All specificities take the form of "calls," but insofar as specificities inherently propel us to the universal they call us to be responsive to the "should" as such: they call us to acknowledge our own character *as called*. They call us to bear witness to our own nature as witnesses.

The nature of our situation, then, is to call us to fulfill it—to turn most fully toward its needs—by fulfilling ourselves—by turning toward ourselves. Indeed, this is very much the insight of Socrates in Plato's *Apology of Socrates*, and *Crito*, who sees justice—the attitude of rendering to each what it is due—as the proper maturation of the human individual. As we saw earlier in our discussion of the child, our situation begins as a site of the nonisolability of others, self, things; it calls for its own "end" in something analogous, namely, a situation in which turning to ourselves and turning toward others and things are the same turn.

We are witnesses by nature, and this means we are vulnerable to the call to witness to our own witnessing; indeed, this is the natural fulfillment of our "education." This witnessing to witnessing is responsibility. Let us now consider this witnessing to witnessing.

Witnessing

In an artwork, form (as such) emerges from the determinacies of stone, pigment, sound. Like any thing or any situation, the artwork *is* an epiphany of form; yet beyond this, it is precisely an epiphany *of this fact of epiphany*. The artwork displays, demonstrates, performs the emergence of meaningful form beyond the confines of determinate specificity. The artwork, in other words, manifests witnessing: it is witness to witnessing.

Ethical action, that is, action that is motivated by the call to duty, is action that has its own character as witness in its grasp and answers to this. To act ethically is not simply to realize a determinacy but to realize it *because one should*, which means one is acting in light of the recognition of one's character as called. The action, in other words, bears witness to one's character as witness.

Philosophy, too, is such a witness to witnessing. Philosophy is description and metaphysics, but description and metaphysics as artistic, ethical action. Philosophy is description in that to learn can only be to learn about reality as it is revealed to us. Reality is epiphanic form. Reality educates us by showing itself, and it exceeds its preconditions. It thus cannot be deduced—only described. Philosophy is metaphysics in that it is motivated by the effort at witnessing to the very nature of this epiphanic form. Philosophy is a critical discipline inasmuch as its careful attention to description of epiphanic form reveals the inadequacy of various presumptions about the nature of things. Indeed, as we saw earlier, our responses to our perceptual situation are typically one-sided, suppressing the ambiguity of form that has many compelling aspects in favor of only one (very real and very compelling) facet of things (such as the Bacchic favoring of the immersion in the absoluteness of the local circumstances over the detached appraisal of the universal principles of the whole community of things, or the Apollonian favoring of the availability of things to intellectual clarification over the experience of things as an inconspicuous platform for everyday life, and so on). Philosophy, as rigorous perception, is, on the contrary, precisely the attunement to this ambiguity of compelling form. Rigorous description is metaphysics, for it is witness to the very nature of reality, that is, it is witness to the witnessing of epiphany as such.

Such philosophical witnessing as descriptive metaphysics is itself artistic and ethical practice. To describe form is to describe its character as calling forth actions, that is, to describe reality as it is is to bear witness to its imperative nature. Description must itself be prescriptive, a call to action. And it is a call to action via investing into expression the very epiphany of epiphanic form, that is, by engaging in transformative expressing, that is, art. Philosophy is descriptive metaphysics as ethically transformative expression.

We have considered the emerging "how" and "who" of our experience and have seen that our very nature as witnesses (a nature that is typically misrepresented in describing us as "consciousnesses," "subjects," or "knowers" in a narrow sense) is such that it grows into fulfillment in its witnessing to its own witnessing. This fulfillment of our nature is found in art, in ethical practice, and in philosophy. We will proceed, in the remaining chapters, to consider these three: art, ethics, and philosophy. We turn first to the domain of ethics.

PART 2

◆◆◆

Bearing Witness

4

♦♦♦

Responsibility

On Ethics

We are humans inhabiting a human world. That world is not the one described by the physicist or the chemist, nor even the rich world of life described by the biologist. The physicist, chemist, and biologist all describe a reality stripped of characteristics that are inherent to the world of our experience. Our reality—the human world—is a world of ambiguity, of infinities, of oughts. Our reality is the reality of people engaging with people, and the world fundamentally exists for us as the context for the development of that interhuman life. We will now explore further the dimensions and dynamics of our interhuman world, of our experience of other persons. We have considered the inadequacy of philosophies that try to understand our experience of other persons based on a reductive model of experience as a kind of information processing. What, on the contrary, is the form of the epiphany of the other person? What is the bodily rhythm it induces? The epiphany of the other as a person is experienced as the erotic, as the ethical, as the invasive, as the friendly; we encounter the other in experiences of shame, of betrayal, of love, dignity, and honor. These terms define the reality that is interhuman life. To share the world—to co-witness—is to bear witness to the epiphany of the erotic, of betrayal, of respect, and so on. It is these dimensions of experience that we must describe if we are to comprehend the form of our interhuman reality.

Sexuality

Erotic experience is the fundamental bodily recognition of the presence of another person as a person. Erotic attraction is the stirring of the other

73

in me, in my body. In our bodies we bear witness to each other and to our bodily reality. Another person carries within him the world: he is immersed. He exists as the enacting of *this* situation. And so do I—I "exist" the same world. And yet in him the world is folded otherwise than in me. The other is me—my world—but folded away. The other person is experienced as a strange presence, a presence that remains absent from me in its core: though we are both "here," the other seems located elsewhere.

With the family member, it is typical not to notice the otherness of the folding, the elsewhere of the other person. As family members we tend to live as if we formed a single fabric, as if for both of us there were an identical "here." Of course there are great tensions in family life, and of course such alienated individuation always lurks and typically develops to some significant degree (and, to be sure, many erotic situations do in fact develop between family members), but the epiphany of "family member" always carries with it a nonindividuation that keeps such people from assuming fully the experiential reality of "other person"; (indeed, the threatening character attributed to incest is rooted in this fact that the erotic relationship is at odds with the definitive character of family relations, as is the fact that children typically find their encounters with their parents' sexual behavior troubling). Erotic experience is the encounter of one developed human person with another: an encounter of nonfamilial aliens.

In our full-fledged encounters of "person to person," the elsewhere of the other fold is definitive of the experience. That they are elsewhere can make others seem trivial and unworthy: a bus driver, a merchant, and a waitress can all be dismissed as irrelevant because they do not share my here. Their detachment can be an excuse for responding to them as mere things (a trivializing of the other reminiscent of the blindness of familial piety). But the elsewhere of the other also can be experienced otherwise. Erotic attraction is the experience of the pull of the other's fold. Erotic attraction is the epiphany of "other." This other is not a family member. This erotically recognized other is not a trivial thing. The other experienced as other is a new kind of person above and beyond these two; indeed, the other experienced as such redefines what "person" is. The other draws me out beyond the comfortable familiarities of my here, as in the case of the protagonist of Laurence's *The Fire-Dwellers* who is drawn out of the tight confines of her family life and into a sexual affair and a changed autonomous attitude by the free-spirited man she encounters. The other elicits my self-transcendence, elicits my learning, elicits my agency. In erotic attraction, the other is the voice, the emblem, of my own nature as being-beyond-myself.

It is not surprising that we associate the emergence of erotic life with adolescence. Of course this is rooted in the body's transformations in puberty that allow the reception of the rhythm of the sexual other. Of course, too, there is a nascent sexuality at play throughout our childhood development and within our family relations. But there is something distinctive of adolescent sexuality beyond childhood sexuality, and a reason for it beyond physiology. It is in adolescence that we first begin to develop our independence, making the transition from family life to adult life. This is the entry into the human as such. This is the initial experience of the other *as other person*, with all the strange possibilities—all the creative, self-defining possibilities—that this entails. Erotic life is witnessing to the emergence of the call of the other. In our burgeoning sexuality we experience the birth of humanity within us as the epiphany of sharing, that is, *freedom* as co-definition.

In erotic experience, I experience the other stirring within my body, just as I find myself—my reality—in that other, calling me (that is, I experience that other *as* my reality, my future beckoning to me). It is not given what this erotic tension, this bond, will mean, what it will *be*. It is as a free—a detached, "elsewhere"—being that I am called. The erotic other calls me out of my static routines, calls me to be a unique, singular agent—calls *this one*, this body, to act. How I shall act is up to me: it is not prescribed, and it is no one else's to perform. The other, likewise, as *that singularity*, is the one who must engage with me. It is *up to us*: this is the core of the erotic experience. In erotic life, we feel the reality of sharing, of original, creative co-action.

Sexuality and Responsibility

Our erotic perception ranges everywhere—our sexuality is a dimension that permeates all our experience—but its enactment is a condensation of focus and charge in single realities, in individual "things." Our erotic perception draws us to a focus on individual persons in their detachment from others. In erotic attraction we are drawn by a particular individual who (at least temporarily) is definitive for us of erotic attractions. As we have seen with the exemplary powers of our bodies for initiating us into the experiences of power as such, and the exemplary role our family members play in initiating us into humanity as such, so are single individuals exemplary for initiating us into the realm of erotic life and the realm of "others" as such, realms that are themselves inexhaustible, realms characterized by possibilities that will always exceed the finite experiences through which we apprehend them. Erotic attraction, though, is not the apprehension of a "rule" or an abstract concept of "other." It is precisely the experience of the absorbing character—the "metaphysical magnetism"—of a single individual in all that person's complexity and determinateness, and with all the possibility that emerges from that specificity. That other person defines for us what it is to be desirable, becomes that to which all else answers. Single persons become for us paradigms of what attractiveness and desire are.

Similarly, our erotic life singles us out as unique individuals. *I*, this body, feel desire, and I, in my singularity, elicit erotic interest from others. This experience of the other is thus also the epiphany that "I am this body," that is, the recognition of the independence of my singularity as defined by my bodily determinacy. The compelling epiphany of the singularity, the "absoluteness," of this other is equally the experience in which my own absoluteness as a singular being *and* the fact that I *am this* body are compellingly manifest to me. Our essential, reciprocal, embodied singularity is definitive of the experience: my erotic interest in another is the desire that my attraction for this other be welcomed and reciprocated by this other, which is the desire that that other be desiring my desire. The erotic epiphany is the epiphany of us as *these specific ones* jointly desiring our mutual desire.

The emergence of erotic experience is the emergence of our sense of ourselves as individuals: individuals free to create a shared community with other individuals. Erotic experience is thus the experience of freedom. And this experience, this freedom, is from the start "co-," that is, it is an experience accomplished with another/others, and not in metaphysical isolation. Erotic experience is this experience that draws us beyond the community of family life into our life as independent individuals, and yet this latter experience is itself a communal experience, an experience essentially defined by and dependent upon our shared experience with others.

In my erotic desire, I desire the other's erotic interest in me. It is here that I *feel* myself to be folded toward the other; I feel that I live within the experience of another, that I am subject to being someone in a way that I cannot control. My body is responsive to your desires, your perspective. I experience your body as calling me to touch it, and I experience my own body as calling out for the touch of yours. This "being drawn to touch" is our most familiar sense of the erotic or the sexual, and we are most familiar with thinking of this touching as kissing, hugging, genital intercourse, and so on. Actions such as these are, of course, essential to our sexuality, but in fact they underrepresent the richness and complexity of the erotic sphere. Touching is, to be sure, only a reality for bodies, and these practices all seem quintessentially bodily. The body of sexual life, though, is not inert matter, but is my body *as me*, and your body *as you*. In myself-as-a-body I experience the call to be *with* you-as-a-body. For this reason, what it is "to touch" is a much more complex matter than our familiar images of sexuality suggest. Let us think about the notion of touching.

Typically, when we think of touching, we imagine two bodies up against each other. We ask, for example, "Is that cup touching the book?" We mean by that, "Is there no measurable gap between the material limits of the one thing and the material limits of the other?" Such a spatial continuity, however, is called "touching" only equivocally, for neither the cup nor the book *encounters* the other, neither *feels* the other. When we speak of touching another person, we mean *to feel* that other and *to be felt* by her or him. It is only because we are the kind of being who *can encounter* that touching is a possibility for us.

This notion of encountering or feeling, however, points to the essential "foldedness" of our immersed-detached character, the essential way in which our bodily determinacy is itself already something experienced by ourselves, something each of us is taking up for ourselves. *What it is to touch your hand*, for example, is thus not reducible to a simple spatial continuity to the limits of our bodies, not reducible to an abstract rule about what it is to touch hands, nor reducible to my experience of your hand: what it is to touch your hand cannot be defined without reference to you, and what it is *for you* to be touched. Inasmuch as I want really to touch *you*, then, I must find out *from you* what that requires. I, on my own, cannot make it the case that I touch you, that what I intend, so to speak, is what you receive. It is only because we are folded, only because we each exist as a self-aware perspective, that touching is *possible*— whereas neither the chair nor the table can touch another—but this very condition that makes it possible for us to touch one another also makes it in a sense impossible, inasmuch as the fact that you are folded otherwise will always leave you in some way "eluding my grasp," so to speak. My touching, that is to say, always aims at you precisely as a reality that is "elsewhere" to me. We make our two bodies collide in space, but even in sharing this same spatial here, we each are this "here" folded otherwise.

In sexuality, we desire to touch the other. We typically resort to simple and obvious means—kissing, caressing, and so on—but these practices fall short of fulfilling the erotic impulse. Indeed, we can easily find ourselves alienated from our partners rather than sharing an experience with them when we do not feel gripped by their touches. A kiss can be alienating and invasive, uncomfortable and unpleasant, as much as it can be a welcome embrace, and, indeed, the very fact that one's partner presumes that such a gesture will surely be welcome, without actually finding out one's own views, can itself be what is alienating in the experience. Because I desire *you* and you desire *me*, and because you and I are immersed-detached folds, our desire to touch can only be fulfilled through communication.

At the most immediate levels of bodily touching, we must find out from our partners whether they find genital intercourse or holding hands desirable or whether they find these practices repulsive: we must find out from them what touching is to them. Only from you can I find out what the touch is that you desire—I cannot determine this on my own, nor can any rule of nature or culture, physiology or psychology answer this in your place. Touching, in other words, is never "immediate" but is always mediated by the perspectives of the persons involved. This inherent nonimmediacy to touching, this fact that it is the other *person* we seek to encounter in and through the bringing of our hands or mouths into contact, entails (1) that those acts of caressing are always *gestures*, that is, *they express our desire* to touch the other rather than simply accomplishing that touching, and (2) that these familiar attempts to touch are not the exclusive routes to touching but are only the most immediate routes we adopt. We often hear, for example, that some thoughtful gift or gesture was "touching," and we can easily feel caressed by someone's words or glance or general attitude of attentiveness more so than by someone's manual manipulations of our body. Like "grasping," and the other notions we considered in chapter 2, "touching" is itself a bodily meaning, the very nature of which is to open itself up beyond its immediate form to a broader and richer realm of meaning. Our desire to touch the other is ultimately a desire to have our experience of the other (and of ourselves) be shared with that other's experience, to have my experience really come into contact with yours.

In sexuality, I, as a body, experience the call to be *with you*, as a body, and thus, in erotic life, we experience our bodies as the locus of the communication between us, and the site of our answerability to each other's perspective. In erotic experience, my experience of my body is of this dialectic of mutual answerability. Indeed, this is why our sexual life is so intimately intertwined with issues of shame, pride, and self-image, and equally with questions of "right and wrong" and "good and bad." Erotic experience is fundamentally the experience that *who I am for you* matters to me, and our erotic life is our negotiating with this experience.

This erotic attracting—like bodily determinacies, artistic expressions, and family life—is an originary initiation into meaning. Erotic experience reveals humanity *as humanity*, as self-creative co-witnessing, as active sharing. How we will go on to be human will be how this epiphany is elaborated in our subsequent experience through our own creative action. Because of the essential creativity of erotic life, erotic life is a domain inherently characterized by issues of responsibility and initiative.

Other people will elicit from us erotic attraction: other people, qua *other people, are* invitations to creative co-definition. We are accustomed to imagining ourselves and the nature of humanity as already finished and defined, such that our human interactions are just so many ways of combining and actualizing the possibilities that have already been fully mapped out. In fact, however, our own and humanity's definition(s) are always subject to redefinition and reinterpretation through our creative action. There is no pregiven map for who/how we can be. Eros *is* the experience of this: it is the epiphany of the openness of our nature. We do not, however, always accept to "dance" to this rhythm of co-creation. Indeed, we have already seen in general that our own self-perception is typically at odds with our reality. This also is true of our erotic life in particular.

Another person solicits my interest as I solicit the interest of that person, and these solicitations are mutually reinforcing (a dynamic nicely dramatized by Thomas Nagel in his essay "Sexual Perversion"). How we answer to such calls is how we define ourselves and how we create for ourselves and for each other a human reality. With another, we make a bond. It is a bond rooted in our bodies rather than in our self-conscious theories. The bond, like an act of expression, will be our way of behaviorally claiming ourselves, our way of saying who we are. Some bonds are more honest, some less, some more informative, some more concealing, some open to richer development, some more limiting (a situation well described by John McCumber in chapter 4 of his book *Reshaping Reason: Toward a New Philosophy*). Through our bonds with each other we can express the richness of our freedom, or we can unite in an effort to conceal our humanity. The character of the bond will be manifest in how we behave rather than in what we explicitly assert about ourselves. Let us consider some such bonds.

In another I can feel a kindred spirit, anxious like me to hide from all truth, and we can bond in our project of self-deception and the refusal of freedom. Alternatively, I can bond with another through our shared recognition of the excitement of learning or the weight of responsibility. In you, I can find an opportunity to express my sense of my unrecognized importance, and I can use you as a site for domination. In me, you can find a justification for your view that you are always misunderstood and abused. Between the two of us, we can establish an expression about ourselves that we mutually reinforce, by which we settle ourselves into a self-perpetuating system of self-deception and dishonesty. We can agree that we are the chosen pair, special in insight, and all others simply demonstrate their ignorance through their failure to see and do things our way. Or, on the contrary, we can support each other in our senses of ourselves as creative individuals constantly relearning who we are through our embrace of new possibilities, new responsibilities. All of these are forms of realizing the epiphany of the bond, but they differ dramatically in the way in which the response to the call of the bond shapes its reality. Let us consider two examples of such situations.

A young man grew up in a family context in which he was largely ignored. This resulted in his growing up into an isolated, prematurely singularized world in which he mostly had only his own fantasy, rather than the supportive companionship of others, to guide and to entertain him. In his family life, his hopes and expectations of others were repeatedly let down, and this led to the development of a habitual way of living that is excessively self-referential. As a young adult, he does not commit himself deeply or trustingly in dealings with friends, and he holds himself in an overly authoritative position for determining how to evaluate situations. His companion was regularly subject as a child to "corrective" treatment by others (parents and older siblings) that purported to be moral and authoritative but was in fact petty, arbitrary, and self-interested. This irresponsible behavior by authoritative figures led her to grow up distrusting the critical judgment of others and to become strongly self-reliant in her pursuit of her interests. For different reasons and in different ways, both of these people are predisposed to disregard the import of criticisms of others and to consider themselves to be in a privileged position to determine the state of things. In fact, this couple does meet critical judgment from others: the people with whom this couple deals do find their behavior defensive, and they feel themselves to be treated by this couple as playthings to be manipulated in their private world, rather than as friends meaningfully involved in their lives, and those friends are thus critical of the couple's behavior because it is unkind and unconstructive. Both partners in the couple find themselves confronted and irritated by the seemingly unrelenting way in which others find this behavior unsatisfactory.

The challenge that this couple experiences in their dealings with others could be taken up as an invitation to self-criticism and self-development, but it could equally be taken up as an enemy to be denied recognition. In his companion, the young man in fact finds someone who is firm in endorsing his behavior as it is—indeed, she reproduces such behavior herself—and with her he can thus form a secure world that repels any potential incursion by the "critical" behavior of others. Their own sense of themselves is that they are rebels, whose nonconformity to the standards of others marks their own greater insight into the way things should be. We saw earlier that we seek recognition from others in order to confirm our own sense of the propriety of our own behavior—of ourselves—and in this situation the young man opts to "feed" himself on his partner's confirmation rather than turning to the input of others as the appropriate gauge for assessing his actions. This "opting" is not simply a self-conscious choice, of course: his partner's perspective is a kind of magnetic force, and he feels himself encountering something real—discovering how things really are—as he dances to the rhythm of her companionship. This is nonetheless a decision, though, for the perspectives offered by the others also are an invitation, and the embrace of them would equally lead to a revelation.

In bonding to form themselves as a shield against the perspectives of others, this couple enacts a fundamental denial of the self-transformative possibilities—and imperatives—of their interhuman situation.

Here we can see the way in which our bearing witness is itself creative, that is, it is a non-necessitated giving of oneself over to an attraction where that giving itself contributes to the performative enactment of the reality to which one is committing oneself. Here we see this enacted as a bond between kindred spirits that is a defensive retreat from the realm of self-transformative openness (a structure also apparent in the couple described in Edward Albee's play *Who's Afraid of Virginia Woolf?*). The couple could, however, generate a radically different situation here. They could find in the critical responses of their companions a friendly and welcome route into a way of living that would be healthier for them both. We can see an example of a healthier and less defensive enactment of a bond in another couple.

Two women, both recently separated from longtime companions, explicitly find in each other the opportunity to approach an erotic relationship differently than each has done in the past. The first woman was pressed to "succeed" in order to secure a "good job" and a "good husband," and, though very intelligent and enthusiastic and recognized to be such, she was typically encouraged to adopt a subordinate role to her male "superiors," first by her family members and subsequently by her former romantic partner. From her new companion, this woman draws encouragement to pursue daunting projects, as well as deriving a sense of legitimation for her sexual desires. She experiences her relationship with her new partner as offering her a new liberation in her relationship to her own body, and she takes this as well as an opportunity to cultivate a greater frankness in her intimate interactions with her partner and a greater openness in her public expressions of affection. In all these respects, it is her own sense of agency that is highlighted and supported in this relationship, and the fact that this is the actual "theme" *of* the relationship further encourages her taking the initiative to, and taking up the responsibility for, shaping the relationship well. The second woman grew up with parents who were very concerned about their image in the eyes of others, and she found herself under pressure to look and act in a way that would reflect well on them. Her own rebellious attitude toward what she experienced as the oppressive regime of her family life led her to cultivate her own popularity initially with her adolescent and subsequently with her young adult acquaintances. The companionships she developed were founded on the basis of her commitment to doing whatever would make her popular, a strategy that led her to feel empty and like a failure. This woman, who sees in her new partner a figure of strength and talent, derives a heightened sense of her own worth as a person from the fact that she is highly esteemed by her companion, and highly esteemed not for her ability to play the role of a "good date" but for her intelligence, emotional depth, and sense of commitment. Her greater sense of self-worth in her relationship with her new partner further encourages this woman to cultivate healthier and more substantial relationships with others outside the relationship. Both find their relationship as well to be a site for engaging responsibly with larger social and political concerns, seeing their own relationship as a public gesture about the nature of relationships, their same-sex relationship remaining a challenge to prevailing norms of "compulsory heterosexuality," as Adrienne Rich calls it.

In this couple, we can see the erotic bond being taken up as a site for growth, as an opportunity for strengthening and opening the connection with the richness of the world, rather than as a bulwark against the incursions of the threatening outside. Indeed, the creativity inherent to their performing of the bond is itself used to cultivate that very creativity, to magnify the responsible agency of each partner singly and of the couple as a whole. It is worth noting as well that for this couple it remains true that their entry into their relationship is a kind of "defense" in that it is a withdrawal from the world of their former lives. It is not "defensive," though, in that it is not premised on the interpretation of the outside as an enemy, and, correspondingly, it is not closed in its relationship to the world. The embrace of the relationship by the couple as a protective shelter is not inherently bad but is, on the contrary, much of what is of value in erotic relationships: indeed, this is the primary way in which one is empowered to move beyond the constraints of the "piety" of family life. The real issue for assessing whether the relationship is healthy is whether the form of our response is true to the nature of the reality made available in the erotic epiphany, whether the trajectory of this self-contained unit—the self-defined bond of the couple—is open to or closed against self-transformative growth in interaction with the epiphany of reality offered up by the world.

The Growth of Interpersonal Responsibility

In our erotic bonds we shape our humanity: we shape who we ourselves are, and we project a vision of what humans can be. It is in our erotic life that we are called to be singly responsible for realizing our co-creative essence: our erotic life is our interpretation of the essence of humanity. We can thus see here that how we create and shape our bonds is one of our deepest ethical issues (an issue generally ignored in most discussions of ethics, which focus, typically, on what are taken to be the acts of isolated individuals or else on issues of social groups beyond the realm of the interpersonal). Our erotic life is not so much a set of "acts" that are objects for judgment by moral values established elsewhere as it is the very site where we embrace our essence as "responsible," the site where we enact our most basic ethical stance. Inasmuch as sexual life is the domain in which we creatively and performatively embrace the sense of responsibility, there can be "morals of sexual life" only insofar as this reality of human experience sets up within itself criteria for self-interpretation. Just as reductionist empiricism cannot do justice to the reality of perceptual life, neither can an imposed code of sexual mores do justice to the self-creative reality of sexual life. Sexuality *is* our life with other people. *It* defines the parameters of human meaningfulness—of human reality—hence it alone can be the soil within which morality grows; it cannot be defined and judged by some moral code constructed elsewhere. Such a code would tacitly draw whatever value it does espouse from the creative power of the very sexuality it seeks to limit. Let us consider the emergent, self-interpretive norms of sexual life.

It is from erotic life that the epiphany of responsibility emerges. I witness to my own character as witness-to-another's-character-as-witness: it is the reciprocal witnessing that essentially defines that realm. In erotic experience, (1) I find myself folded away from myself into others, while simultaneously being called up in my ineffaceable, absolute singularity: my reality is answerable to a source beyond myself, where (2) that source is itself characterized by answerability. This inherent answerability that characterizes both me and the other, then, entails that erotic experience is always pulled toward an infinite answerability, that is, *it does not find an unambiguous resolution in any single person or any single thing.* Erotic experience is the discovery that I am beholden to the reality of others, which ultimately means that I am beholden to reality as such. Let us investigate these matters further.

As I allow my erotic perception to be locally focused, and I absorb myself in the absoluteness of the other by whom I am attracted, I see that all that matters is to do what he wants. This—the other's desire—becomes my highest ideal, the source of my freedom. I want my actions to be what he desires—to be desirable to him. The other, though, is a *person*, and has a person's needs, a person's desires. Like me, the other person expands beyond himself and has a need to grow, to learn, to develop: the other is himself a witness. Like me, the other is much more beyond what he immediately takes himself to be. While I may initially build my freedom through answering to the arbitrary whims of the other, I am, through my erotic experience, opened up to a richer, more demanding experience of the other. My freedom comes through this other who—inasmuch as he is deeply characterized by inherent needs, demands, and possibilities—himself opens me up to criteria, principles, and demands that exceed his immediate whims. To care for him ultimately will mean to go beyond these immediate whims and, indeed, to *judge* his whims according to *his* best interests. I must become the agent of his better judgment if I am indeed to care for his person. Loving the other requires caring for his health; it requires caring for his education, relationships, and future. Ultimately, I must bear witness to his character as witness. Being answerable to him ultimately means making myself the agent of his answerability to himself. My initial focus on his immediacy leads me to his human core, leads me to the judgment of that immediacy by its own higher internal standard. Here, then, we see the emergence of a norm within the terms of the erotic bond.

My erotic perception also can lead me to focus not on the immediate local detachment of the other, that is, on the way he exercises in his whims his ability to treat immediate circumstances as optional, but on his immersion. I can be drawn into his world and the desire to care for him by caring for it. His involvement in school can lead me to an embrace of the subjects he studies, or his involvement in music can lead me to an embrace of music. But to move to his world is to move to the embrace of values that are not simply defined by him in his immediacy. Here, the thingly determinacy of his world now sets up norms within my erotic attachment to him. This side of erotic perception leads me to respect and care for a world in a way that can actually lead to a criticism of and opposition to him to whom I was initially attracted. I may find, for example, that he is mistaken in his approach to his studies, or that he is neglecting his music, and, on behalf of his world—that is, on behalf of him qua immersed—I may oppose his actual behavior.

Indeed, these two paths through the immediacy of the other to his immanent norms are correlated. We saw earlier that intensification and extensification of experience are coordinated: the other's *inner* richness *is* the richness of his *world*, his situation. In fact, as I am drawn in my local focus to a greater emphasis on my other's real, internal needs, my perception is naturally being led out into his world. Similarly, the care for his world will lead to the recognizing of principles for determining his reality and his real needs beyond how that appears in his immediate expression of his desires. Erotic attachment to the other naturally leads to the growing perception of the ambiguity of that other, which means the ambiguity by which that other both is what he "is" and is also the possibilities by which he exceeds himself; which means the ambiguity by which he both is an exclusive individual and is the world; which means the ambiguity by which he and I share and do not share an identity; which means, in sum, the ambiguity of the performative unity of things, others, and myself. To identify these dimensions as ambiguous is to remind ourselves that the various senses involved here are in tension with each other, and that there is not a clear-cut answer to the question of how to love the other. As much as we can undervalue the self-transcending character of the person in favor of his immediacy, we also can undervalue his immediacy in favor of "the universal"; and, of course, inasmuch as our apprehension of the "higher" needs of the other (and of ourselves) depends on our judgment and insight, our sense of the other's "best interests" can be misguided. The erotic dynamics of interpersonal care are the most tender and the most demanding of our interhuman negotiations. Erotic attraction properly points to its own development in our mutual education into the nature of caring for each other.

From both sides of the ambiguity of erotic perception then—that is, from the side of the independence and detachment of the erotic object and from the side of its immersion—there is an inherent motivation to grow beyond the immediacy of the erotic attraction to a more mediated, educated eros in which what grows is a recognition of the *real*, inherent needs of a person and the values of a shared world, and these two values, further, are coordinated. The natural rhythm of erotic attractions is to grow into an epiphany of the value of the interwoven needs of the world and of persons, that is, the experience of responsibility. Erotic experience is the key to our education into responsible humanity.

Sexuality is not "animal," and it is not "amoral." It is, on the contrary, the originary matrix of interpersonal humanity and responsibility. Its development, further, is precisely toward the recognition of the ultimate coalescence of these two notions: humanity and responsibility. Our freedom is our openness to the experience of others that can grow into the simultaneous recognition and realization of this identity. Sexual life is our participation in the call to grow, the call to learn, the call to become ourselves through creating a shared experience of the respect for our mutual worth, an experience that cannot be separated from a respect for the worth of the world.

The Ethical Field

Erotic experience is experiencing the other as a person in and through experiencing oneself as a person. This epiphany of the other is the foundation of ethics: ethical life is the field of reality revealed to us in our openness to the phenomenon of the human, in our openness to the reality of witnessing to our witnessing of the other as witness. Erotic bonds are the content of this ethical field.

In all our experience, our freedom is the field of possibilities opened up to us by our immersed determinacy: our freedom just is the situation's own powers of self-transcendence. The hand, for example, is an aspect of my determinacy (a specificity in which I am immersed) that affords me

various powers of engagement—various specific ways of being open—
that are precisely my freedom, the empowering of me to transform my
situation. Our bodily capacities particularly enable us to build upon ourselves: our powers are recursive—self-reflective—such that we can turn
our powers upon themselves and expand them into new horizons. The
body's folding upon itself is its capacity for self-transcendence.

Similarly, our human substance—our very reality *as persons*—is
found in the determinate human bonds we enact. It is the specific others
with whom I become fused that define who I am. They define me, however, as do the determinacies that are my organic body: they define the
horizon of possibilities that I am, that is, they are my doorway into a dynamic future rather than merely a static "settling" of who I am (though I
may, indeed, bond with them so as to resist this future and to effect just
such a static "settling").

Our erotic bonds are our doorways into human meaning, human
values. These portals have the same Janus character that all determinacy
has. These bonds both give me a specific value—a specific commitment
to a specific other person—and launch me beyond that specificity into
the larger field of human value as such. Erotic relations launch us into a
world of values to which those relationships themselves become subject:
erotic relations are themselves self-transcending or—the same thing said
otherwise—they are self-subordinating to a value that emerges from
them. Let us consider this dynamism a bit further.

Ethics begins in the thoroughgoing throwing of oneself into the project of being *for* the other, and in general "loyalty" is the most immediate
form of ethical life. We have already seen (in the preceding section) that
this loyalty has its own inherent trajectory of development, whereby my
loyalty to the other transcends my commitment to his immediacy. Here,
though, we can see another trajectory of self-exceeding that lurks within
the erotic bond. Indeed, the very value revealed in the epiphany of another person stands as a challenge to the project of loyalty. This is because inherent in this project of being for the other is the inescapable
need to be a detached individual oneself: the value of the loyalty comes
from *my* being loyal. The project of loyalty thus rests on a necessity to
maintain the integrity of oneself, even though the project of loyalty does
not as such acknowledge this. Similarly, the very ability to recognize the
other's wonderful personhood is found only in my being similarly such
a person. Thus the dignity and worth revealed in the epiphany of the
other's personhood must similarly inherently characterize my own personhood. The project of being simply for the other does not do justice to
the epiphany of the other person, for it is not a project that affords sufficient recognition to the necessary, and necessarily worthy, personhood
of the loyal lover. The erotic experience is an epiphany that thus has

within itself the motivations to develop beyond its immediate self-abasing form into a form of engagement in which one's own individuality is recognized, maintained, and respected. Loyalty to the other thus transcends itself in commitment to an inherent mutuality of human value.

The erotic bond, then, is by its nature the epiphany of an "ought" in the experience of the other *as* to-be-loved; at the same time, however, this experience itself gives rise to values that entail a criticism of this original stance, for the very logic of the project of exclusive loyalty to the other demands that I not be exclusively loyal to the other inasmuch as I must be loyal to myself as a precondition for fulfilling this project. The erotic experience thus throws itself beyond itself, throws itself beyond its immediate form into an embrace of a value that exceeds and challenges the original value. This is the Janus-like, self-transcending character of the erotic bond as an ethical experience.

Ethical experience just is the experience of the human. Our ethical reality is always determinately rooted in the specific bonds by which our humanity has taken shape: ethics is the demand for loyalty to these bonds. This loyalty, however, cannot simply rest with the immediate loyalty that is the thoroughgoing sacrifice of everything to this other or these others: rather, ethics is the commitment to these bonds by being committed to the reality of the values to which they give rise. Our lives are rooted in our bodies, but they are not simply focused on our bodies. Rather, we live *from* those bodies *into* a world they open. Similarly, our erotic bonds open us into a world of human value to which we are beholden; they are doorways that direct our focus away from themselves. At the same time, we cannot be in the world at all except insofar as we preserve and care for our own singular, organic determinacy, for ourselves as discrete individuals. Similarly, the human world is open to us only by our caring for the specific bonds through which it is revealed to us.

Ethics, then, like perception, carries the twofold ambiguity of locality and universality. Our erotic bonds will always be local human situations calling for our commitment in the form of responsibility to the specific dynamics and demands of the specific determinacy of those bonds. They will also always lead us into the values of the human as such, into the realm of principles, rules, and laws for accommodating the dynamics and demands of the human in general. We will always be drawn both into the realm of impersonal principles and into the realm of personal loyalties. Also, like perception, ethics is characterized by the ambiguity of self and other: the very experience of the erotic other gives rise to the imperative to respect myself as an ethical value. We are thus answerable to three absolute values: you, me, and all of us, that is, our immediate loyalties, ourselves, and the human in general (each one of which, qua immersed-detached, both points us to a distinctive realm of "subjective" autonomy and equally opens up a distinctive world to which we are responsible).

In our nature we will always find ourselves answerable to these different forms of ethical imperative—the imperative to the local other, the imperative to oneself, and the imperative to human value as such. We will stand condemned by these realities any time we pretend to be answerable only to any one. Each of these three "roots" of ethical experience is a source and principle for criticizing our actions if they answer only to another of the roots too one-sidedly. Successful ethical life is the successful navigation of this threefold imperative form: supporting, and not betraying, this threefold system of commitments.

Honesty and Betrayal

The bonds between us are real. We neither begin nor end as metaphysical isolates. Our reality as persons is always interwoven with the human as such, and especially with the reality of specific others. There is an epiphany of love, an experience of a reality between us that exceeds any self-conscious choice or action either of us has made. Indeed, marriage is as much a discovery of a new human reality as it is a decision made by the participants. In love, in marriage, we experience again something like the membership we experienced as children in family life. Here, however, there is a difference. Love and marriage are phenomena of the adult world, that is, of the world of individuated freedom that has emerged through adolescent erotic experience.

Love and marriage are extremes in this experience of the bond, because they are thoroughly individuated (that is, they are relations that pertain exclusively to the individuals involved in their singular specificities) and because they are all-embracing, that is, they are pervasive and comprehensive within each person's life. These are precisely erotic bonds that have become thoroughly extensive through their thoroughly intensive embrace of the other. These bonds are real—to experience them is to bear witness to the birth of a miraculous interreality that is *us*, even as it exceeds what either of us could be singly—but they are not the only real bonds.

Whenever we engage with others, new realities are given birth, new interhuman spaces emerge that we can inhabit. Friendship, like marriage, is a reality, and so, of course, are the sexual and romantic bonds that are not monogamous marriage but are not friendship. And so too are the bonds of professional organizations and workplaces, churches, classrooms, and sports clubs, when these are built on a kind of belief in, commitment to, and membership in the institution as opposed to simple labor for a wage or something equivalent. We tend to assume that these occupational associations are purely "contractual," purely "accidental" to our own proper reality. In fact, though, there are significant ways in which it is through these and related associations that we become human.

We assume business and professional relations and the like to be merely contractual because we typically devalue the significance of work. Work is typically imagined to be a burden, forcibly imposed on our natural leisurely condition; in part, this is, as Marx showed, a consequence of the structure of wage-labor that characterizes modern capitalist society. In fact, though, it is in our work that we forge our bonds with the world, and thereby forge our own identities. In work, I enact my reality as an agent, or, better, I prove my reality as an agent. Agency is not something automatically present in a human individual, nor is it located exclusively in that individual; agency is itself an accomplishment, and it is located in a bond between self and world. My powers are what are allowed or afforded by my situation. Those powers can, further, be turned back upon the situation to further their own development, and this process (of practice, of education, of habituation) results in a transformation of the situation and what it affords. It is through our effort—our work of answering to the demands of operating with the determinacies of the world to accomplish our desires—that we build a situation in which we have self-determining powers. Through our work we learn about ourselves and our abilities by enacting and developing those abilities, and we learn about our world through engaging with and transforming that world. Through our work we create a world situation that reflects back to us our own sense of agency; the world of our work becomes for us our mirror, our self-consciousness. This is the source of the profound satisfaction one finds in work, as Faulker describes in the case of "the convict" in *The Old Man*, who particularly relishes the sense of self-reliance he acquires when he has the opportunity to work at hunting alligators for himself rather than engaging in the familiar drudgery of prison work (pp. 106–108). Our work is thus anything but trivial—it is where we bring our developed selves into being.

Our working engagement with the world is one situated within a shared space; we work on a world inhabited by others, and we work with the support of others. Our working development of a self-world bond is equally the development of an interhuman bond. It is for this reason that our collegial and professional bonds in our workplaces, classrooms, and sports clubs are by no means trivial and peripheral to our identities but are essential elements of its scaffolding. The social relations of our workplaces are typically very important sectors of the arena of our humanity. Of course, as Marx, again, showed, these important arenas can be cared for better or worse, can be supported or hindered by others, and the workplaces of most modern people are designed in deeply unhealthy and unfulfilling ways. What this means is that our human development is significantly impoverished in these very important dimensions. And, of course, the fact that our general cultural outlook downplays the importance of these dimensions further works against our taking what actions we can to maximize the fulfillment these relations could bring. Though the lesser intensiveness and extensiveness that typify these associations do indeed indicate that they have a status that differs from that of a marriage or a family, they remain species of the same genus, requiring analogous input and producing analogous effects, and they need to be analyzed according to the same logic. Like the banality of ordinary language, which conceals the transformative dynamism of artistic expression, the banality that characterizes the bulk of our dealings with others (like the ordinariness into which marriage, for example, typically develops) conceals the explosive dynamism of erotic, expressive life that lies at their basis.

There is, then, a multiplicity of types of bond constituting for each of us the determinacy of our ethical field. It is common for us to think that all of our human relationships can be classed as the familiar types "family member," "friend," "lover," "associate," and, indeed, to derive an ethics on the basis of this (i.e., if you are not "x," then you must be "y," and you must behave in the way appropriate to our expectations about "y": "You are not my girlfriend, so you must be only a friend, and therefore kissing cannot be appropriate" is a familiar example of this). It is indeed true that there are real and important ontological differences between these types of relationships, and that each marks out a distinctive human co-reality; nonetheless, this familiar taxonomy (1) is extremely restrictive for analyzing the possible forms of human reality, and (2) suggests that these essences are fixed and predelineated, where in fact *each* of the four types just mentioned (family member, friend, lover, and associate, but also the myriad others not included in such a list) is really a possibility and an invitation for creative invention of what it will be. Similarly, the different forms of relationships give birth within themselves to criteria for their evaluation and for their own development, and it is such internal criteria to which one must turn for developing an "ethics" of human relationships rather than invoking an independently established "law" for that "type" of relationship. Each form of relationship is a form of commitment, a form of co-witnessing, and brings with it its own distinctive responsibilities, and ways for measuring success or failure in living up to these responsibilities. "Good" and "bad" amount, roughly, to "support" and "betrayal" of these commitments, of these bonds qua ambiguous, qua open.

Bonds are real, and bonds constitute a "we." This means that we are real only in a shared way: our reality is not, strictly speaking, solely our own. For this reason, betrayal is also a reality. A bond is a sharing, a co-witnessing.

In a bond, we give up our exclusive possession of our own reality: what we have is only "ours," not strictly "yours" or "mine." In this sense, my own reality is entrusted to you, and yours to me. In our shared reality, we are inherently vulnerable to each other; indeed, it is only as mutually vulnerable that we realize our humanity. Betrayal is dishonesty about this fact of our shared trust and vulnerability, of the sharedness of our reality. Betrayal is pretending that what is "ours" is simply "mine" or "yours." Betrayal, that is, can take the form of theft—claiming what is ours to be solely mine—or refusal—claiming what is ours to be solely yours. Betraying is my accepting the trust of your reality and then not acting in a way consistent with this trust. We can betray family members, friends, colleagues, and spouses. Whenever there is a bond, betrayal is possible; whenever betrayal is possible, there is a bond. If betrayal of the bond is dishonesty about the fact of coexisting, then support is honesty. Before addressing the theme of honesty, let us look further at the place of betrayal within the reality of the bond.

Our adult lives are constituted by a complex interweaving of bonds: the bonds of love, friendship, collegiality, family, and so on. These bonds constitute the substance of our lives, the substance of our personalities. But these bonds are all realms of co-ownership, all shared domains. This entails that our very personalities are cooperative, communal ventures. This means that others—our others—have legitimate claims upon us, upon our very identities, that in all the domains of our action, we are answerable to others with whom we share that domain. We typically live in a comfortable reliance on the harmonious compatibility of these domains. Doing so, however, requires that we consider ourselves sufficient authorities to decide how each of these domains has an impact upon us, that is, we decide for ourselves the priority and relative placement of these bonds. The very shared nature of these bonds, however, entails that the authority does not reside in the individual alone to make this decision. Consequently, our very personalities are sites of legitimate interpersonal conflict.

I may, for example, be a mother, a high school teacher, a Catholic, a wife, and an Italian American. Each of these ways of describing *me* in fact describes an interpersonal or social *relationship*, a *community*. Each of these dimensions of my reality, too, is characterized by "oughts": each makes demands upon me, and inasmuch as these domains are *me*, these are demands placed upon me by my own identity, not by an alien source. Though in many situations in my everyday life these different realms of my reality coincide harmoniously—indeed, are mutually supportive— I also will regularly find myself in situations that call upon me to decide which is "more really" me. I may, for example, care for my sick daughter rather than preparing my lessons for my students, and I may refuse to

participate in various sexual activities with my husband because they conflict with the demands of my Catholicism. Typically, others feel betrayed
by actions such as these; and even without another feeling betrayed, the
conflicts between one's bonds are real. Indeed, even if such decisions
never provoke obvious interpersonal crises, such a presumption of personal authority to set priorities is unavoidably and constantly at play in all
of my ongoing affairs. In all such situations, hence in the very enacting of
my personality, I arrogate to myself the authority to decide the disposi-
tion of the various shared dimensions of my reality, yet I do so in possible
(and, ultimately, necessary) opposition to the preferences and trajectories of the others who legitimately share those realities. Just as we saw earlier that the norm of loyalty has its own betrayal built within its very logic,
so we can see here that the sharedness of bonds has nonshared, personal
appropriation built within its very logic. A form of betrayal, then, would
seem not merely to be made possible by the reality of the bond but to be
made necessary. Let us consider how or whether this is indeed a betrayal.

What we are seeing here in this conflict of bonds is a further consequence of the ambiguity of identity that we studied in chapter 2. The very
nature of any thing is that its own identity opens onto the larger realm
of the real as such, and we, as witnesses, are therefore drawn in two different directions: we are drawn into the greater density of the thing itself
as a unique individual, and we are drawn beyond the thing to the
grounds upon which it rests and the wholes within which it is comprehended. We have seen, too, that our erotic ties to individuals draw us
into the unique absoluteness of that individual and beyond that individual to the principles and communities upon and within which that individual is based. The conflict within our bonds is founded upon these
same ambiguities. Our personal decisions about how we will appropriate
the shared realms of our identity will be the decisions about the "level,"
so to speak, at which we will apprehend the identity of each bond. Our
decisions will reveal the extent to which we accept the uniqueness of a
given bond as absolute—therefore leading us to subordinate all else to its
"magnetism"—or the extent to which we subordinate the significance of
an individual bond to a more universal structure within which it functions. The form of betrayal that we just determined to be inherent to
these bonds, then, is in fact just another way of seeing the ambiguity of
the bonds. Inasmuch as the absoluteness and the relativity of the individual are both real, the "betrayal" we are seeing here is in fact a kind of
honest apprehension of the reality of the thing.

In fact, then, the decisiveness with which we must appropriate our inherently conflicted personal identities is perhaps not so well called a "betrayal," or, at least, it is only ambiguously such. What we might more truly
recognize here is that the bonds themselves, precisely because of their

inherent ambiguity, demand our creative, performative appropriation of them. I can never simply "be" you, and so our bond, as much as it is a shared reality, also is necessarily a site of distance and nonidentity. It is for this reason that divorce, for example, can as legitimately be a witnessing to reality as marriage can be: divorce is by no means obviously a betrayal of the marriage bond but can easily be an attempt to do justice to the reality of that bond. The only circumstance in which I would not be called upon personally to perform a decision in which I resolve the ambiguity of the relativity or absoluteness of my bond to you would be the (impossible) situation in which I were you; such a situation, however, would precisely not be a *bond*, would not be *shared*, but would simply be a self-identity. Indeed, to call our appropriation "betrayal" is to reinvoke the norm of simple loyalty that we saw earlier to be inherently problematic. Simple loyalty and simple betrayal are typically thought of as opposites, but in truth loyalty cannot really be separated from betrayal, for truly being loyal requires exercising judgment, in the sense of the setting of priorities that involves contextualizing the one "absolute" with respect to others, and in the sense of determining what is its best interest, above and beyond the immediate way that the other may portray its own interests. It is nonetheless worth preserving some sense of the notion of "betrayal" here, though, because these gestures of loyalty can legitimately be judged to be betrayals *by the other*, even though they are gestures of support. If we treat "loyalty" as the term for absolute, self-abasing giving of oneself to the other, and if we call these responsible commitments to a bond that necessarily involve a betrayal of such absolute loyalty "support" or "commitment," then we can see that there is no way of taking up a commitment that does not involve risk, no guarantee that one has apprehended the right way to support the other. What we are seeing, then, is not so much that we cannot support our bonds as that the reality of a bond cannot be understood without the definitive difference of personal appropriations inherent to it. Beyond such constitutive and therefore unavoidable "betrayal," however, there is a deeper betrayal of the bond. Betrayal in this deeper sense is found in the denial of the bond that it is a bond, that is, in the pretense that the bond is simply a self-identity, something not realized as decisive, performative, personal appropriation.

Betrayal, in this deeper sense, can take different forms, each of which is a way of pretending that the bond is not a bond. One way—the way we identified earlier that takes the forms of "theft" or disavowal—is to act toward what is our shared reality as if it were mine alone, or as if it were yours alone. What we have just now been seeing about the necessary role of personal judgment and decision allows us also to see another form of betrayal of the bond that often masquerades as responsibility to the bond. This second form of betrayal is the attitude that pretends that a bond does not require judgment and appropriation, that it is not ambiguous and shared but is an obvious, settled piece of reality. This form of betrayal is the one we studied earlier that argues, "Since we are 'x,' it follows—without reference to the way you and I inhabit the bond—that 'y' and 'z' must be done." This is an attitude that reifies the bond and severs it from the intersubjective engagement that is its very content and meaningfulness. This is the attitude that imagines that "marriage" and "friendship" must take a specific form, specifiable universally and necessarily for all persons regardless of their particularities, that it is "obvious" that a sexual relationship with someone other than one's partner is "cheating," or that children should always be concerned about the well-being of their parents. In fact, the ambiguous, tender essence of our bonds calls for a sensitivity and an openness that rejects these simplistic approaches that hold the bond and individual apart.

Caring for the bond—responsibility—requires embracing the unpredictable and self-transformative character of these interhuman realities. Here, Aristotle's discussion of the ethical "mean" in Book II of his *Nicomachean Ethics* is especially helpful. Responsibility—honesty about our bonds—will always require a kind of courage, a stance of active and vulnerable commitment in which one exercises one's best judgment to determine what is uniquely appropriate to the unique situation, rather than resorting to these different "easy" stances that falsely substantialize and isolate the individual and the bond. In the "Melian Dialogue," Thucydides presents the Athenians as saying, "You seem to forget that if one follows one's self-interest one wants to be safe, whereas the path of justice and honour involves one in danger" (*History of the Peloponnesian War*, book V, 107). Though the context we are considering is the personal relationship rather than a political policy, the same principle holds true: the demands of our bonds will always require us to step outside our comfortable frames of reference if we are to be truly open to preserving their human essence.

There is indeed such a thing as honesty, and there is indeed such a thing as betrayal, but honesty with respect to our bonds will thus never be a simple matter of loyal obedience. Honesty will entail living in light of the ambiguity inherent to the bond, living in light of the inherent necessity that I personally appropriate what is necessarily ours, and that you do the same. Betrayal most fundamentally will be living under the pretense that this is not so. Being true to our bonds will always require judgment, will always require decisions from which our personal creativity—our personal appropriation—can never be separated, and honesty will require the recognizing of this ineffaceability of our appropriation, our responsibility. Honesty is enacting this appropriation *as* a witnessing to the situation. Betrayal is appropriation that holds itself exempt from such a responsibility to bear witness.

Universality and Property

We have found the epiphany of humanity in the erotic sphere. In our discussion of the ethical field, we saw that, within the erotic sphere, there naturally emerge the values of loyalty to a specific other, of self-respect and of responsibility to the universal, each of which has its own internal dynamism. Just as our ambiguous relationship with things impels us in different directions that can never be "ironed out" into a fully resolved and uniform experience, so does this multivalent erotic answerability result in a human experience in which our commitments do not admit of a simple resolution: erotic life means that we are called in multiple and different ways to assume a number of different identities, and the bonds that characterize these relational identities are themselves ambiguous. Let us pursue further the specific character of the identity we are called to in relation to "the universal." We saw earlier the need for our identity as "individual" to emerge from our identity as "family member," and we also saw the limitations of the abstract notion of the individual and the need to recognize the fulfillment of our identity in the role of "witness." In our discussion of our (erotic) responsibility to the universal, we will simiiarly see both the essential place of the role of "abstract individual" within our human experience, and, ultimately, the need to transcend this in the open stance of witnessing.

Inasmuch as answerability to the single other (loyalty) naturally gives rise to answerability to its grounds (responsibility), the answerability inherent to the erotic sphere naturally gives rise to answerability to universal humanity in general. Such universal responsibility is the reality of answerability to all others in principle and therefore to those others with whom one does not have immediate personal bonds, and this answerability therefore entails relating to others qua representative of the universal rather than qua unique. Such an answering to others as such is therefore a recognizing of oneself and one's fellows (both distant and close others) as *examples of* that to which one is answerable, and it is thus an embracing of the imperative to responsibility to others as a "formal" notion: it is the necessity to judge distant others as well as those with whom one has personal bonds and, indeed, oneself by the same standard. The attitude of universal answerability, which is a naturally emergent form of responsibility, is therefore a responsibility that can (at least in part) only be realized formally, that is, responsibility must in part take the form of a code of action based on formal principles of what it takes to give justice to another person as such, *any* other.

Here, once again, we see an engagement with specific examples of something giving rise to the pure notion of that thing, in this case, the answerability we experience to specific others inherently giving rise to an answerability to others as such. Our erotic experience of the compelling character of the singular other led, through answering to the immersed-detached character of that other and also to the experience of oneself as necessarily folded otherwise, to a growth of experiences of responsibility, including a responsibility to humanity as such. It is thus ultimately from the erotic impulse—an impulse initially committed to a single other—that the experience emerges of the need to answer to a universal humanity in which each person is an indifferent "one." This is the natural emergence of law as a witnessing to the demands of the epiphany of the other. Law is thus an erotic reality, a developed phenomenon of the field opened up to us through our body's erotic openness to persons. Let us look further at law and related realities to see both the essential place of law in our experience and its limitations, and to understand more fully the propulsion to universality in our experience of others.

In referring to law as an essential aspect of human experience, we should not understand law simply as the explicit rules we posit to regulate behavior. The phenomenon of law is much broader than that. Law in general is the inherently human phenomenon of the community defining itself. The understanding of communities as thus ultimately self-governing is the primary meaning of "democracy." (Indeed, that democracy is simply identical with the notion of human self-governance is why, ultimately, Marx says, in his "Critique of Hegel's Philosophy of Right," "All forms of state have democracy for their truth" [89].) But the ancient Greeks, who largely introduced the explicit embrace of communal self-determination into our history, themselves especially emphasized the ways in which the laws that are the principles of their self-governance are not exclusively products of self-conscious choice: law also is tradition and custom, the "unwritten" form of behavior accepted as normative by a community and passed along through ritualized or other noncognitive processes. As Pericles says in his famous funeral oration, quoted in Thucydides' *History of the Peloponnesian War*, "We obey the laws themselves, especially those which are for the protection of the oppressed, and those unwritten laws which it is an acknowledged shame to break" (II, 37). These "unwritten" laws are the customary beliefs held by a community, preserved and remembered in the practices of reenactment of the traditions. Sophocles' *Antigone* is a classic portrait of our experience of such laws and as that tragedy makes clear, these traditional laws—often mapped onto naturally occurring differences in our bodies, in different expectations for how men and women should behave, or how people with different skins colors should be treated—provide a meaningful orientation to our lives that functions outside of the parameters of our explicit, reflective decision making. Inasmuch as we grow up in and into them, these unwritten laws are the irreducible terms in which our social relations are articulated. Very much as the family is the "given determinacy" by which we establish an identity, so are these laws, the resources by which our identities are formed, the very substance of our social lives—indeed, the families into which we grow will themselves typically be participating in some such laws, and we thus imbibe the laws, so to speak, in imbibing our mother's milk—and, as the inaugural terms in which we live, these also are the terms through which we can be open to change. In referring to law as an essential dimension of our human experience, we must remember that the laws by which communities govern themselves are both the self-consciously devised policies for public behavior and also the traditions that have spontaneously developed and been reproduced and reinforced (for better or for worse) through collective practice.

But whether "written" or not, what makes law "law" is its universal, binding character. Though the law itself may not acknowledge this, its ability to function *as* law rests on the experience of the single individual recognizing himself or herself not as a unique individual but as one of a type. The laws may require me to recognize myself as "a wife" or "a man" or "a half-breed" or "a foreigner." And even if the laws in question explicitly attempt to define people in terms of specific, determinate types (such as different laws for men and women, or different laws for peoples of different skin colors), those laws implicitly rest on a deeper and more generic identification of the person as a representative of the universal: such laws *all* rest on the inherent ability of each person to experience herself or himself *as* law-bound, as the kind of person who (1) can be an instance of a type and (2) can embrace an identity that answers to the universal. In other words, even if the law *explicitly* marks me as belonging to a specific group, it *implicitly* marks me as belonging to the universal group that can live under law, and in that sense even those defined by different laws as different "types" more fundamentally belong to the same "type" by virtue of being law-bound. In our earlier discussions, we saw the way that our inherently open nature always propels us beyond whatever limits we try to impose to "fix" or settle our identity. Here in our discussion of law we now see an analogous way in which laws that try to restrict our identities to settled "types" themselves, by their very nature as "laws," point to their own need to transcend themselves in a properly universal conception of humanity.

The very form of the laws that would serve to lock people into closed groups based on identifying some feature of their bodily determinacy as essential to fixing their identity implicitly points to a need for the perspective embodied in those laws to transcend itself and to recognize a community of persons beyond the exclusionary boundaries those laws explicitly define. From a new angle, then, we are here seeing again the phenomenon we studied before in our discussion of the emergence of the detached individual from the matrix of family life, for to experience law is to live in the demand that I am "one," answerable to the same code as all, an individual, equal as such to all other individuals. To move beyond the family is to move into a shared human world, and though this typically means moving into a social world shaped by particular customs and "laws" that reproduce a closedness of interpretation of human possibilities that mirrors the narrowness of the familial vision, the implicit nature of that social, legal world is to point to its own fulfillment in a properly shared world: a universally shared world experienced *as* universally shared. To experience the world in this way is to experience oneself as one person among many, answerable to the same universal as the rest, which is essentially the notion of equal participation under the law.

The experience of oneself as a legal "one" thus marks an important development in our identity. It remains insufficient, however, to accomplish our answerability to the universal dimension of our human reality. This inadequacy can be seen more clearly if we consider the development of the individual specifically in relationship to the corresponding notion of the development of one's "property."

Property and erotic life are closely related. As a child growing up in a family, one is not initially a "possessor of property" beyond the power one can assert over one's own organic body (itself a contested zone in the power dynamics of family life, as well as being a relation of property that must be accomplished by the child). As the child grows, however, her developing individuality is both supported and recognized by her growing possession of her own things. The child begins by forming an identity as a family member, that is, as immersed in her immediately given others. The possession of property is part of the process of growing into an individuated, detached personhood, the personhood whose full-fledged birth occurs in the emergence of erotic life—a birth that is pointedly the person's removing of her single organic body from family jurisdiction and putting it where she wants, giving it to the other(s) chosen by herself, thereby demonstrating that it is "hers." (This is the *gesture* to the family field of asserting her own possession of her own body, as well as the enactment of that possession through entry into the world of chosen human bonds.) It is this postfamilial, erotic individual who becomes as well a legal "one," an equal participant in a social space governed by law: to be such a responsible individual requires one to be "self-possessed," to be individuated as a self-responsible body. The property of this erotic, legal individual is more, however, than simply the individual organic body.

Property is that in which our identities are realized. My reality is the powers that arise for me from my determinacy. Something is my property to the extent that it offers to me its powers, to the extent that I realize myself through it. My property is thus fundamentally realized as my organic body—the hands, joints, eyes, and tongue that have my will as their reality, that give themselves over to me—but it also is realized in further determinacies to which that organic body gives access. Though initially the pencil is an alien object, through practice I come to inhabit it, and to live through it, and the coupling of my hand and the pencil becomes a medium that allows the realization of my thinking (in the words I write) and my artistry (in my drawings). Indeed, through my regular practices of cleaning the dishes, doing laundry, and mowing the lawn with a push mower, I come to accomplish a new relationship to my dishes, my food, my clothes, the mower, my lawn and, of course, my limbs and my organic bodily functioning in general. We saw earlier that "my" powers can equally be described as the way that the things of my world give themselves to me, and we can here see the body-world coupling as the emergence of a new "giving," a new "affording" of power to me by the world. Through these *practices of engagement* I realize myself, and I do so in a way that is simultaneously a responsive caretaking of the things of my world and that is equally a giving of itself on the part of the world. In this way, these things become my property, my proper embodiment.

For the growing child, its sense of itself as a detached individual is an essential dimension of its growth, and that means its sense of nonidentity with others must be developing. Distinguishing "me" from "you" is integrally interwoven with distinguishing "mine" from "yours"—my action, your action, my arm, your arm, my space, your space, my toy, your toy, my prerogative, your prerogative, and so on. In having personal possessions, one has a sphere of influence in which one's will is authoritative, and growing into the experience of oneself as a fully fledged individual agent in the world involves experiencing the differentiated spheres of influence that come with ownership. The child's developing sense of its autonomy will typically involve not just the experience of its body as its property but also the experience of a (growing) range of other things that it is empowered to dispose of according to its own will and over which it therefore has responsibility. These possessions will, again, meaningfully function as property if it is through engagement with them that the child grows into its inhabiting of its world.

Through all of these practices of engagement what one is doing is coming to be an agent. Indeed, in the absence of these practices or similar, the world would remain for me an alien place, and I would remain ineffective in dealing with it. It is through these practices of engagement that I inhabit the world—it becomes *my home* rather than an alien arena—and it is through this inhabiting of the world that I become an agent. My agency is embodied in these things and their giving of themselves—of their powers—to me. In this way, they become my property, the proper embodiment of my agency. It is through these practices that the world becomes my own: my world, my home.

But inasmuch as another person is just a folding otherwise of my own situation, the property in which I am immersed also will be the determinacy through which she realizes her reality. For this reason, property will always be contested, not in the sense that people will enter into dispute about it (though of course that is true too), but in the sense that it is metaphysically ambiguous with respect to its "being owned" or "being appropriated."

We share our world: it cannot ultimately be divided and apportioned among us. All of us realize our humanity through appropriating *the same* world. The same holds true for the things of the world. Each thing by itself is a metaphysical magnet, something that, in its absoluteness, subordinates all reality to itself as center, and cannot be separated from the fabric and texture of other things. Things are not real *by themselves*; the localized individuality of each is itself realized only by claiming for itself the reality of all other things. Consequently, things cannot be severed from the texture of reality and handed over to one person or another: their very nature will not allow them to be taken out of play within the total texture of things that forms the medium for others' self-realization. Property is a reality, but inasmuch as *the same world* is the property of each of us, the fundamental phenomenon of property cannot be a division or an apportioning.

This notion of something proper to me that is also shared is familiar to us when we think of our inhabiting of places. We make ourselves at home in a city, in a region, and in a country. A city is "mine": my home. I develop my identity through investing myself in the city environment, making it offer up to me its riches, appropriating it such that its identity becomes mine: I am a citizen of Medan, a New Yorker, a Roman, and so on. The city becomes my city, and I can reveal this city *as* I appropriate it—I can reveal *my* city—to another. In making the city mine, however, I do not take the city away from others. Indeed, the city just is the vast multiplicity of diverse ways of appropriating the city. Each Parisian has her own Paris, and Paris just is the total—or, rather, infinite and inexhaustible—phenomenon of this multiple appropriation. Similarly, I can be a prairie dweller or a Southerner, a Peruvian or an Eritrean, in each case living an identity that is inseparable from my "proper" place without thereby limiting the availability of that place to be home to others. As a home, a determinate, worldly reality— a place—can thus be multiply owned.

Further, our world is not just a natural setting of things situated in space. It also is a world with a history. We live in a human world that is itself defined by time, by memory, by tradition, and by history. As we come to adopt/accomplish our identity as human persons, we witness our participation in a tradition of human identity, find ourselves participants in a world itself revealed to us as shaped by past human ventures. This legacy of human history is not more mine than yours, not something that can be carved up and divided out among us. As with all property, all things, we can make history more or less "our own" by taking it up, "enowning" it, or ignoring it. But to enact such an appropriation is not to seize a portion of it: it is to "take up history's call" and to make ourselves the inheritors of its significance. Such possessing, such "owning," does not diminish history's continuing universal availability.

Of course, we are very familiar with the ways in which we do take up our property—our things, our homeland—in an exclusionary and oppositional fashion. While it is important and indeed necessary to practice a protective concern for the determinacy in which our identity is realized, this should not be confused with an exclusionary self-enclosedness that is used to oppose and oppress whatever is alien. Whereas it is essential to preserve for ourselves (rightly) an ability to be "at home" and to live as "one's own" self, and whereas it can be essential to stand in defense of one's homeland and culture, as the Greeks did at Marathon and Thermopylae, and as the Cubans have done for decades in the face of pressure for the United States, we often (wrongly) treat ourselves as unchallengeable masters of our own domains, and in our wealth or our "patriotism," we use our power over our property to oppress others (very much in the way family membership and simple loyalty fail to acknowledge the worth of what is beyond their own immediate sphere). If we return now to the notion of law (and from there ultimately to the notion of language), we can see the problem internal to this attitude of "mine versus yours" or "us versus them."

The laws that govern our human environment are exemplary realities that are enowned by each of us but are never diminished in their universal availability by this appropriation. In principle, my recognition of the rightness of the law, and my "living in" the law such that it affords me liberation and fulfillment, does not stand opposed to your similar appropriation; rather, it demands it. Law is a reality that can be appropriated *only* by sharing. In these cases of making our laws our own, we enact a *nondivisive* appropriation, that is, our owning of this reality does not diminish its availability to being owned by others.

The crucial character about law here is that it is *universal by its very nature*, that is, one "enowns" the law *only if* in taking it up as one's own one takes it up as a common reality and, indeed, as an *imperative to* that commonality. In experiencing myself as living in the law, I experience myself as answering to a shared standard, that is, I experience you (insofar as you too belong to this community of law) as having the authority to judge me. In other words, I experience my very identity as legitimately in the hands of others. To live in the law is thus implicitly to recognize one's beholdenness to the endorsement of others. The nondivisive ownership or appropriation of law as a kind of shared property thus goes hand in hand with the experience of oneself as inherently involved with others.

This phenomenon of nondivisive appropriation of shared property is manifest in works of art in a way that is particularly important for revealing the ethical imperative inherent to property, and it is perhaps most recognizable in works of literature. An artwork—a sculpture, a musical tune, a painting, or a book—is not simply a thing but an epiphany, and this reality is only realized through an engagement with our responsive body, that is, it is only realized through, in the example of the book, a reader reading. The experience of the book-as-art, that is, as epiphany, comes through the process of reading, but it is not exhausted in this activity. The identity of the book enters into one's very self—through the effort of reading one has appropriated the book—and it lingers, it reappears, and it resonates in and structures future experience. One comes to experience *through the book*, through the powers its determinacy of expression have afforded one. A book one has really appropriated—a book that one finds to be articulating one's very self—typically is so important to one that one wants to share it. The nature of the epiphany is that one wants another to witness it as well. Our possession of this book feels inadequate if we possess it only alone. Indeed, the book seems inadequately realized if it is read by one only. The book *needs* to be shared to be real, to be itself. *I* can possess it *only if* others can too. When another does read the book, that other can likewise appropriate the epiphany and likewise live through it, but this does not in any way diminish or divide the book nor inhibit its capacity to offer up its powers to another.

In this phenomenon of enowning/being owned by the artwork, we see the character of a taking in that is simultaneously a propulsion outward. I make the artwork mine only as the imperative that it be yours as well. Like the law, the artwork is something that cannot truly be possessed—cannot be possessed *as* artwork—if it is possessed by oneself alone. To own it personally, one must own it *as* something to be shared. Unlike appropriating the law, though, in which we appropriate it as something the sharedness of which is already presumed, appropriating the artwork precisely calls us *to accomplish* the sharedness. Whereas the law speaks from a (presumed) community of identity already established, the artwork speaks of a community to come. This intertwining of property and universality that we see in art and law has its most fully developed form in language.

Personal property as shared reality is ultimately and most fully realized in our language, itself the ultimate medium for our humanity, our co-witnessing. Our experience of each other ultimately rests on expression—art—and the system of mutuality of expression that it makes possible—language. Our entire human reality is lived in the sharedness of language, of a system of articulation in and through which we can express ourselves—our most intimate personal uniqueness—even as the system enables the equivalent self-expression of others. In our words, we speak our own minds, we explain ourselves to ourselves, we appropriate our whole reality. But this is done through a system that is defined by its *necessarily* shared and public character. It is only *by being shared* that language can be personal.

Language is meaningful—is language—only insofar as it can be taken up by others, repeated in contexts other than the unique one in which I utter it. It is this shared character that allows it to *say* something, and that thus allows me to say something to myself. As we grow into a language, we grow into the ability to give voice to ourselves, to articulate ourselves to others and *to ourselves*. Our language is thus the medium of our self-apprehension, our self-reflection, our self-experience. Because we thus dwell in language, our very establishing of a personal life is something that is done in the medium of shared meaning. Our participation in language, then, is our inhabiting of the very experience that "mine" must be, in principle, "ours," that individuality emerges only in the context of sharedness, that the experience of "one's own," of the most specific, personal, and intimate, draws its life and meaning from an essential indebtedness to what is "ours." This character of the experience of language reveals the ultimate political imperative that is at the heart of our experience. To discern this political imperative, let us reflect briefly on the different characters of these different forms of shared property.

In our places and our histories, the shared reality we appropriate nondivisively is itself specific and contingent, and to appropriate these realities is also to mark ourselves as belonging to this or that specific community. With law, however, the reality we appropriate is, in principle, universal. Though it is true that different cultures will always have different laws—both the "unwritten" cultural customs and traditions and the explicitly legislated statutes—the ultimate idea behind law, as we saw earlier, is the idea of the "indifferent" individual, that is, the person equal, in principle, to any other. For that reason, it is implicit to all law as law that its aim be universal: the very conception of a law-governed people, in other words, is inseparable from a project of universal humanity. The formality and indifference inherent to law thus mark out an essential dimension of our lives, a real aspect of our identity to which we must bear witness. We can see that by itself, though, this "take" on our reality does not do justice to our nature. Law is based on the insistence *not* to recognize the weight of the specificities of how we each as singular selves inhabit our situations: law, on the contrary, precisely requires that we evaluate our relationships on the model that we previously deemed "betrayal," that is, it disregards the tender ambiguity of particular identities and relationships. Just as we saw earlier that we are essentially familial, but that the family reality is not adequate to our nature as persons, so too can we here notice that belonging to a society of "legal persons," though again essential to our reality, is ultimately inadequate to it. It is in art and language that we find the interweaving of uniqueness, specificity, and universality that adequately answers to our ambiguous and self-transformative nature.

In language, we are precisely impelled to *communicate,* to make experiences of sharedness where they did not exist before. Unlike laws, which hold us to predefined rules to which we and our situations are required to conform, language precisely reshapes itself to create sharedness *through* the specificities of our unique situations. This is true both in the emergence of the specific activities of everyday communication through which people come into a shared experience and also in the artistic innovations through which the very capacity of our language *to express* is creatively transformed so as to make new forms of sharedness possible. Our inhabiting of specific places, histories, traditions, and so on displays our inescapable specificity. Our living in the laws displays our impulsion toward universality. In our language, we in our specificity inhabit the ongoing event of reconciliation with the specific reality that is beyond us.

Our impulsion toward the "universal" dimension of our erotic identity is realized in different forms. Though the experience of law, and the correlative experience of oneself as an abstract "one," is essential to our experience, it is not adequate to our reality. It is in the universality of art and language—the open universality of a community yet to come—that we find the adequate medium for the realization of our ambiguous identity as "witnesses," and engaging with this reality itself requires us to relate to property in a particular way.

As we have seen, we are free—we are real—only insofar as we are determinate, specific, and embodied as a thingly reality *proper to* us. Our proper powers *only are* the powers of our proper determinacy. The reality of a person is thus inseparable from the reality of property: to be "me," there must be "mine." As our human reality—our freedom—grows, so does our determinacy, our property. This growth of our reality is a growth into a shared identity. Because our identity is a shared identity, this shared identity is itself only realized in and as shared property, which is, ultimately, language. Our answerability to the universal—the sharedness of our identity—is ultimately accomplished precisely in our experience of the things of our world as the site of communication between our identities. "The universal," then, is the imperative to language, and this, politically, is the imperative to pluralist multiculturalism. We will always be culturally specific, but our "human" imperative is to realize a shared world *within* our multicultural specificity, which is accomplished not by appealing to an abstract legal code that disregards our differences but by finding our "proper" realities to be novel sites for communication, that is, language, and that means experiencing *our* property as a material able to give voice *to the other.* This is the ultimate meaning of property as language.

With this consideration of property, we have revisited the metaphysical consideration of the nature of the thing that was our theme in chapter 2. In identifying the reality of property, we are interpreting things as the embodiment and realization of our own identity. What we have seen is that taking things thus as the site for the accomplishing of our co-experience is something to which we are impelled by the very demands of responsibility. Indeed, we have seen, ultimately, that it is only in and as thus seeing things that we are able to answer to that responsibility, because the very medium for the realization of our shared humanity is the world of things *taken as* language.

Let us now complete our reflection on property by taking up the notion of "private" property. The various realities we have so far been considering—places, history, laws, languages—are essential components of humanity: we saw earlier that our human reality is shared, in principle, and in these realities we are seeing the determinate forms of sharing, the determinate forms of a reality that *cannot exist* in "portions." Because these inherently shared realities are fundamental to human reality as such, any distinctively "personal" property, inasmuch as it is a developed dimension of human reality, will have to be inherently dependent upon and derivative of this founding sharedness. To understand the reality of "private property" within this context of our shared humanity, we will begin by drawing out a link between the theme of property and the theme of honesty.

Property and Honesty

The explicit person-to-person bonds of adult life are themselves rooted in the more fundamental bonds of language and law we have just been considering, for we (normally) come together as persons within what is already a shared political and linguistic reality, and these realities can show us further the close overlap of questions of property and honesty. Whenever we speak, we appropriate personally a shared language. That sharedness can be newly accomplished through the use of language, as in the transformative, erotic situations in which one's personal appropriation of language is an artistic act that itself becomes the new shared reality of the bond it forms between us; or, that sharedness can be the already established medium of our interaction, which is the typical use of language in more mundane linguistic situations. In either case, my personal expression has its own meaningfulness defined in terms of the communal bond expressed in the language. All of our linguistic communications with each other are based on a kind of trust and caretaking: our exchanges succeed in meaning something only because we are able to rely upon our interlocutors to preserve the sense of our (shared) language. As soon as we try to make ourselves uniquely authoritative for the meaning of our language, it ceases to be a language, for it ceases to communicate. (The failure to live up to this responsibility is well documented in Book I of Plato's dialogue, *Republic*, in the conversation between Socrates and Thrasymachus.) We can see from this that the familiar "ethical" issue of truth telling and lying is really a subspecies of the deeper theme of honesty and betrayal in general, which is the deeper theme of the metaphysics of the bond, and which is thus closely tied to the theme of nondivisive ownership. In these situations, my words can communicate my personal meaning *only insofar as* they do not aim to "steal" the sense of the language—do not betray the bond—but instead exist as witnesses to the shared sense of our meanings. Our language thus speaks always in (at least) two directions: it says (melodically, we might say) the specific thing I mean, but it also says (harmonically, we might say) that I belong to this community, and that I speak on the basis of its authority. Here, honesty about collective "ownership" of meaning and expressing one's "own" meaning are the same behavior.

This necessary presumption, which underlies all of our mundane linguistic exchanges, of honesty with respect to our shared linguistic reality is paralleled by a similar presumption with respect to the maintenance of our shared political structures. We depend for our everyday ease of action upon the cooperative maintenance of a "public" space in which each of us can pursue her or his own personal projects. This is true in our simple inhabiting of the open air, true in our use of roads, electricity, and telephones, and true in our general comfort with the shared terms of political and social recognition in terms of which we encounter each other. In all of our actions, these shared, historically accomplished, linguistic, legal, and social realities are unconsciously assumed, and our successful interhuman interaction depends on our honesty with respect to these shared realities, our maintenance of them through our actions.

Whenever we speak or act in our mundane affairs, we take our public, shared reality and appropriate it personally, though our personal appropriation maintains that shared reality rather than undermines it. Under special circumstances, we feel called by our situations to creatively transform our shared reality through artistic utterance or politically transformative action, and here too we act honestly inasmuch as our singular initiative is in service of answering to the call of the situation, in service of being its deliverance, an enactment of witnessing, and this will be an action that itself calls to a future community to embrace the revolutionary act or expression and to endorse its propriety. Dishonest appropriation of these situations is attempting to "make the situation" (the language, the political resources, the bond in general) "one's own" in a way that does not acknowledge the sharedness upon which this "owning" depends. Again, then, we see the inseparability of the themes of property and honesty, in that both are defined by their witnessing to our bonds.

These shared realities, these properties of each of us, reveal the essence of property and allow us to understand the proper context for our more familiar notion of "private property" or "personal possession." Private property is a reality and a necessity for persons, but it is characteristically misunderstood by us precisely because it is not understood in the context of the shared co-witnessing of humanity and the Janus metaphysics of determinacy. Privacy and privacy of property *grow out of* our co-witnessing: privacy is a product, not a root. Basically, "private property" in the sense of personal possession and ownership is a sort of realization of language, a way we as a community *say* "yours" or, more exactly, "you." Developing this notion of private property as language, we can now consider this sense of the divisive ownership of apportioned property, but what we have seen already is that this phenomenon itself rests necessarily on the more basic reality of nondivisive ownership.

We have seen that property is essential to our reality, and that it is fundamentally a phenomenon of sharedness. We also have seen, however, that, inasmuch as it is the individuated, detached self of whom this is the property, property also must be exclusive, that is, dividedness is as essential to the reality of property as is sharedness. To understand this, what we must remember is that the very individuality of the person is itself something accomplished only through cooperation: even our most personal life is at root a "co-" experience. What we will now see is that exclusive possession, like personal individuality, is itself a phenomenon of cooperation. Privacy of possession is not an autonomously occurring form of reality but is itself a phenomenon of law, and it is something that exists only as a habit of interpersonal interaction.

We develop habits of private possession and habits of recognizing the possessions of others. These habits are part of the ways that a shared sense of individuated personhood is instituted within a community. The private possessions through which my sense of being an individual is established within a group are in truth the sites of collective support and recognition: it is not that I alone truly possess an isolated piece of reality; it is, rather, that in that thing is condensed the collective support for individuation. The fact that you can invade my house or seize my things makes it manifest that these things have not, in their "being," abandoned their nature as participants in the texture of shared reality; my private ownership is not a phenomenon of them but of us; that is, it is a phenomenon of our human behavior toward each other, and it is the fabric of this that has been violated when my authority over these things is denied. Private possession is the way a community makes a gesture of mutual endorsement in and through a thing. In that thing the sharedness of our acceptance—our witnessing—of "you" is crystallized; your "private possession" is thus a collective appropriation, a harmonization of witnessing rather than a metaphysical isolation of an atom of reality. For me, and the rest of our community, your property is still a site for our own self-recognition, for it reflects back to us our cooperation and our endorsement. Property in the sense of personal possessions—the property of divisive ownership—is thus always necessarily ambiguously individual and social.

For these reasons, then, property and law are closely related realities. The recognition of private property is a collective recognition that individuals are to be recognized and treated as centers of privacy and self-determination. The recognition of private property is the recognition of the formal sense of the person. Thus the imperative toward law and universal responsibility is inherently an imperative toward a collective acceptance—a "social construction"—of the "rights" of persons to privacy and therefore to private property. It is a responsibility of a society—and therefore of persons—to make spheres of privacy for personal practices of self-determination.

Just as it is metaphysically incumbent upon the community to facilitate the growth of autonomous individuals through the collective recognition of their privacy, property, and "rights," it also is metaphysically incumbent upon individuals to recognize the dependence of their "private property" in the shared reality of communal life. The very phenomenon of "mine" and "yours" is a *social* gesture, a *social* practice: my property can be mine *only because* it is ours. Private property—and, indeed, personal individuality itself—is thus inherently responsible to the community: private ownership is *for* the community, that is, it has the norm of social responsibility inherent to it. Not least, then, our analysis of the metaphysics of property shows that most of the ways in which the rights of exclusive possession are understood in contemporary political theory are fundamentally mistaken, inasmuch as the right to personal property and social responsibility are typically construed as opposing realities, while we can see that in fact (1) social responsibility entails the need for private property, and (2) it is only on condition of its beholdenness to social responsibility that there can be private property. The inherent ambiguity of our nature is such that the question of how to discharge this responsibility will always be an open one, always a matter for judgment and decision and not something that any analysis can definitively answer. Indeed, we are always embodied in noneffaceably different bodies, places, and languages, all of which bring their own unique demands; these "exclusive" realities, however, need not be lived in a way that is "exclusionary" but can be lived on the basis of their inherent propulsion toward communication and reconciliation. Our analysis cannot specify in advance a correct answer to the question "How should I act?" in any particular circumstance; what our analysis does show, though, is that to engage with one's private property—whether at the level of one's personal possessions or at the level of one's patriotic possession of a homeland—as if in this domain one were absolved of social responsibility is fundamentally to make a gesture within a shared language, and this gesture is a lie.

Property and Creation

We have seen that the notion of property leads us to the notion of communication; we can equally see that the notion of communication leads to the notion of property. The essentiality of property becomes clear through reflection on the nature of expression itself, and, in fact, the dynamism of expression actually reveals the perfection of property, property's ultimate realization and the fulfillment of its inherent nature. In expression, I embody myself—even as I create that very self. In expression I bring to determinacy my brewing motivations, my very innermost sense of my situation. Equally, it is only through this expression, this "outering," that this sense becomes something real, something substantial. My own self comes to be for me only as this expression—in it and through it. This expression is thus the realizing, the embodying, of my very self. It is my sense that is embodied in the expression: the expression is my determinacy.

This rendering determinate of myself is the creation/expression of myself through the emergence of property. This is because, when I have created in this way, I have given my identity to some determinacy as its essence: it is my work. Indeed, it is me. I live through this my established determinacy. This is, in the truest sense, my property, because it is my expression, not because it is my possession. I rightly recognize myself in the work I have made—in my words or in my painting. (And this is true of the work both in the sense of the creative artwork of artistic expression and, as we saw earlier, in the sense of the products of constructive labor and practices of engagement in general. In all such cases, what is produced is that into which I have invested myself.) I legitimately lay claim to this property, not as possession but as that the reality of which is the revelation of myself.

The very nature of my act of self-expression, however, is that I *utter* it—it *is* an expression only insofar as it is *a public reality by nature.* We have been considering the emergence of private property as the (communally sanctioned) withdrawal from the communal space; here, on the contrary, we see that private accomplishing of property that is precisely the emergence from withdrawal into the community. My self-expression is what is mine in the truest sense, but its very nature is *to be for others*. The property through which I most fully realize my personal individuality is the property through which I give myself (back) to my others.

What we here see about my explicit works of self-expression—namely, that they are mine only *as* calling for sharing—is implicitly true of all real property. Inasmuch as the very reality created or embodied through human work is a human reality, it is a reality *already inherently* responsive to other persons. That means that our human inhabiting of a world is an inhabiting of a human world, a public world, a *shared* world: we are individuals *for the sake of* participating in the shared world. The very way property comes to express and embody our humanity is in its embodying us *as* co-witnesses. Thus the very inherent dynamism of property itself, as of our project of human self-expression and self-development, is toward its recognition as public property, its recognition as the ambiguous medium for communication and co-witnessing. In other words, the natural dynamism of property is toward its perfection as language, our communally shared practice of co-expression and co-articulation: property is language by nature (a communal gesture), and we fulfill it by recognizing it as such and by treating it as a medium of communication. Ultimately, property is that which leads us to others and is precisely the arena for the creative emergence of our erotic life.

Art, Philosophy, and the Imperative to the World

We saw earlier that our erotic commitments naturally project themselves toward single others, toward ourselves, and toward others in general. Since our reality is always characterized by immersion, these commitments always have as one of their sides a responsibility to the worlds of those to whom we are committed. We already considered the dynamic development of commitment to a single other that leads to a development of a responsibility to the determinacies of that person's world. An analogous point can be made with respect to care for oneself. Each of us as an individual occupies a privileged position for protecting ourselves, which no one else can occupy for us, and our discussion of property gives some sense for the specific dimensions of one's own world that call for one to care for them. There is, in other words, a fundamental form of "self-love" essential to the unfolding of erotic and ethical life, and this love in part takes the form of a need to care for the determinacies of one's life—one's body, one's property, one's home. Just as our erotic commitments to single others and to ourselves point us toward the world, so does a responsibility to the world emerge in relation to the commitment to universal humanity.

In relation to the attitude that takes universality up formally (law), for which each individual is an indifferent example, reality is the indifferent setting for this humanity. Concomitant to a (formal) responsibility to a universal humanity, then, is a responsibility to see the reality as this indifferent setting. This is the attitude that is realized in scientific knowing, and this corresponds with some of the familiar ways of taking up the attitude of understanding that we considered in chapter 3. Indeed, we can thus see that the attitude of "knowledge" is, or at least can be, an attitude of taking responsibility—specifically, it is an aspect of witnessing to the universal in humanity. Insofar as formal universality does not, however, offer an adequate grasp of the ambiguity of our humanity, its concomitant comprehension of reality will not be an adequate witnessing to the universal character of real, that is, the "reality" in which humanity as such is immersed. We saw the witnessing to the ambiguity of universality to be realized in the attitude of performing reconciliation in art and language, and, correspondingly, a "comprehension" of reality in these terms would have to be a grasp of reality as such *as* ambiguous. This comprehension—which is what is attempted in this book—is indeed the very attitude of philosophy.

Our discussion of the erotics of human life took us into the realm of ethics, which we identified at the end of chapter 3 as one of three forms of our witnessing to our own witnessing. Our study of this realm has taken us through responsibility, law, and property to language and expression, and we have thus seen that the form of witnessing to our witnessing that is art is inherent to and foundational for our ethical life. Let us revisit now the witnessing to witnessing that is art and conclude with the witnessing to witnessing that is philosophy.

5

♦♦♦

Art and Philosophy

From our discussion of the nature of things, we have seen that one way in which things present themselves to us is as an imperative to experience them in their situatedness with respect to grounds. From our discussion of the nature of persons, we have seen the ethical imperative to answer to the grounds of individuals in such a way as to realize a common human world. From both of these angles, we are seeing that the notion of "reality" is itself a norm, an "ought." In other words, to situate things in their grounds and to see the world as real—as a shared field to which each is answerable as a field to which all are answerable—is an ethical imperative. "Reality" is the "objective" or "thingly" notion that corresponds to the "subjective" imperative of honesty. What, ultimately, is the character of this reality? From many sides we have come to see the attitude of openness and its attendant phenomenon of self-transformation as the essential realities we need to comprehend. We also have seen the essential relationship between art and self-transformation. Let us conclude now by discussing this notion of self-transformation, considering the essential role(s) of art in this process and then, ultimately, considering the implications of this for our understanding of the nature of reality and our relationship to it.

Polytemporality and Self-Transformation

Our study began with reflection on the temporal dimensions of music, or the musicality of lived time. It is in relationship to our theme of self-transformation that these reflections are particularly helpful. In our opening discussion, we considered the musicality of everyday life, the ways in which our meaningful engagement with reality always has a sort

113

of musical structure. Let us revisit this and then consider how this pertains to self-transformation.

Melody, harmony, and rhythm are relative terms, which means they do not name particular things but instead identify *roles* that can be found at play in different things. Roughly, we interpreted rhythm as the indifferent regularity—the repetitive diachronic punctuation and quantitative measurability—of a temporal significance, that is, of a lived engagement with reality. Roughly, we interpreted harmony as the meaningful context—the qualitative character—of a temporal significance. Roughly, we interpreted melody as the specific thread of oriented sequential action of an engagement with reality. These three we called, respectively, the platform, the character, and the narrative of a practice. Let us consider some illustrations.

A *rhythm* could be my repeated structure of a workweek that begins on Monday, ends on Friday, and is followed by the weekend, with its active Saturday and its slow-paced Sunday. A rhythm could be our shared daily rhythm of getting up together, sharing breakfast, parting for the day, reuniting for the evening, and ending the day together, followed by sleep. A rhythm could be the alternation of academic semesters and holiday summers, repeated yearly. Each of these is a (familiar Western) pattern of punctuations, rooted in one's projects, that structures one's life with indifferent regularity and provides the platform for one's multiple, specific practices. Such rhythms can be separately discerned as such, both in our analysis and in our experience. Typically, the rhythm would not itself be what my experience is "about" but would be an unnoticed dimension of my ongoing life. But these rhythms can, however, become explicit objects of our attention: I could like any of these rhythms for itself alone, thus I could enjoy "riding" the rhythmic character of our day as such, I could find the rhythm of the workweek monotonous and oppressive, I could panic about the unrelenting character of the ongoing cycle of my years, we could be frustrated by the clash of our rhythms, and so on. Whether we notice them or not, in all of our actions, these rhythms are being enacted.

The *harmonies* in a life are the ongoing projects that provide the contexts within which our specific actions are embedded. I can be "going to graduate school," "living in my neighborhood," "raising my daughters," "making a home with you," "being part of a group of regulars at a bar," "carrying on family traditions," "being a golfer," and so on. These projects and practices are not so much individual actions I undertake as they are ways of living. They are general structuring contexts to which I become habituated, and they provide the basic qualitative character to my life: in large measure, these are the specificities that define "who I am." Typically, if my husband or good friend asks me "What are you doing?" I will not answer "I am going to graduate school," because this will be very much the already assumed context for my life, and I will answer instead, "I'm getting ready to do laundry," or "I'm paying bills." If, however, a more distant acquaintance I have not seen in years asks me, "What are you doing?" the opposite is the case, that is, I will not think to remark on the detailed specifics of my immediate action but will name the defining qualitative character of my way of life: I will more likely say "I'm working at the hospital" than "I'm trying out a new outfit." Going to graduate school, enjoying the experience of being a part of my neighborhood, or living out my married life with you is typically the settled context within which our more immediate actions make sense. Sometimes this harmonic context has a trajectory of its own, as graduate school, for example, is a project with a beginning and an end that will take a half-dozen years; sometimes, this harmonic context is more static, as participation in a social club has no particular path of development Whether characterized by a progressive trajectory or not, contexts will typically have their own cycles or changing phases, which will be the source of a basic life rhythm. Again, these contexts are separately discernable dimensions of our lives about which we can have attitudes but which typically are presumed rather than thematized within our experience. It is these larger contexts—these "harmonies"—that are carried out *through* the specific sequential acts that make up my daily narrative and that are typically the primary objects of our focus.

It is in and through our individually differentiated actions that these rhythms and harmonies are enacted and realized. These individual actions are the *melodies* of our life, the sequential narratives of our days that are typically the focus of our explicit attention. Making a cup of tea, designing a new business plan, purchasing clothes, answering the telephone, writing a report, daydreaming about a lover—these and so many others are the relatively self-contained episodes of action as which and through which we enact our temporal existence. When we think of "action," it is these relatively discrete practices that we typically imagine. Each such action though is simultaneously an enacting of a larger harmony (or harmonies) and rhythm (or rhythms). Rhythm and harmony are not realities separated from these melodic actions but are constitutive dimensions of any such action. Indeed, if these deeper contexts were removed, then many of our specific actions would lose their point, and we would have no reason to undertake them. It is the harmonic context of our marriage and the rhythm of our daily life together that make my unexpected arrival at home in the afternoon meaningful: if it were not usual for you to be alone at home in the afternoon, or, more seriously still, if we were not involved in a romantic relationship, then there would be no reason for me to come to your house to see you. The action that constitutes the narrative of my daily life draws its meaning from its own specificity, but only in relationship to the larger harmonic character and rhythmic platform of our life.

Let us note, finally, that these rhythms, harmonies, and melodies are as much the meaningful structures of things as they are the meaningful structures of my identity. It is through things that the punctuations of my life rhythms are marked: the changing light and changing temperature of the day or the season, the alterations in the kinds of bird song I hear, the changing sounds of the street traffic, the frequency of telephone calls, the presence or absence of graduation gowns—it is through these that the rhythm of the workday or the school year is tapped out. The harmonic dimensions of my life are similarly embodied in things: the house, the bed, the placement of the decorations, the cellular phone that is always in my pocket, the team jersey in my closet—it is in and through these things that I am in a marriage with you, that I am employed at my job, that I am a participant on the sports team. These harmonies are my way of inhabiting these things, and these things are the embodiment of those projects, those harmonic contexts. Like harmony and rhythm, the melodies of our lives are enacted in and through things. My studying is an elaborate engagement with my library books, the student card that gives me access to the library, my pens, and my notebook. Our going out to dinner is realized through our bicycles, the dinner plates, the door handles, our clothes, the three-peso notes, and more. Again, rhythm, harmony, and melody are not themselves three separate sets of things but are all implicitly enacted through all of the things of our world.

We can see a clear example of this nondetachability of rhythm, harmony, and melody if we consider the latent significance of something that we more typically relate to melodically. My student card, for example, is initially relevant to me at the narrative, melodic level of daily actions in that I use it to accomplish specific tasks that come up in my daily affairs. In later life, however, I may come upon my old student card as I look through an old box when cleaning up my house. The card at that point suddenly becomes a vehicle by which I am vividly transported in memory back to my life as a student. The card no longer has any functional "melodic" significance (just as my example of visiting you at your house lost its significance when the rhythmic and harmonic context of our married life was removed), but its ability to present me with the memory of my own identity as a college student shows that its meaning was not exhausted in that melodic function but was also always its role as a realization of my harmonic identity. I also could have a different but related experience of finding the card, either when I am still a student or after. I may find that seeing the card makes me feel burdened, because it embodies for me the oppressive rhythm of my "daily grind" of going to the library to work on my assignments. Here, again, I am not relating to it in terms of its specific melodic functionality but in terms of its role in enacting the rhythmic punctuation of my life. Our reality is an immersion in the things of the world, and the temporal dimensions of the significance of our lives are thus also the dimensions of meaning that define the things of our world.

We can now use this interpretation of the polytemporality of our world to look further at the phenomenon—the reality—of self-transformation. We have seen that our erotic experience involves openness, and that openness is an openness to experiences of other people and of the world that do not leave one unchanged. Openness is not simply being open to having new experiences "added" to one's life but is rather openness to be challenged by the open. Self-transformation is inherent to the realm of sexuality, and it necessarily involves a dimension of self-criticism which, most importantly, requires the breaking of habits.

There are many forms in which self-transformation can happen in a life. We have identified one such change that is crucial to human development, namely, the transformation of oneself from an identity as "family member" to an identity as "independent individual." This is our most definitive self-transformation as persons and one that, for reasons noted earlier, we never completely accomplish. We also undergo ongoing transformations throughout our growth as children, and there is the possibility of such transformations in the rich dimensions of interpersonal life that ethically and politically contextualize adult life. Let us consider the process of self-transformation, especially its polytemporality, its "musicality."

The specific ongoing dealings I have with the people in my life—with my spouse, my children, my coworkers, the store clerk, the bus driver, and so on—and the specific ways I portray them to myself—rest upon the "map" of interhuman life to which I have become habituated as the basic "harmony" of my life. Throughout chapter 3, we considered the way we develop for ourselves such a "map" of the human world, and it is within this complex web of presumed senses of human interaction that the particular interactions I have make sense to me. It is, in other words, my habitual expectations for possible forms of human behavior and human relationship that provide the basic harmonic structure that supports these various melodies, the basic song structure that each such melody "sings." Because this harmony is a habitual sense, though, it is typically not noticed by me, and if I am asked to describe or analyze my interpersonal relationships, my understanding will typically stop at the superficial "melodic" level, interpreting my relationship only in the terms in which it functions *within* that established harmonic context.

In describing some of my familiar companions, I might, for example, call Ömer a jerk and Davika a good friend, imagining myself thereby to be describing real, autonomous features of them, without recognizing that these perceptions are rooted in my habitual assumptions about how people should behave, about what a friend is, and so on. The very way I perceive Ömer and Davika has a habitual harmony woven into it, and indeed my own perspective is crucially involved in that harmony. What I see as objective features of Ömer and Davika are really implicitly reflections of my own subjectivity: what I see is how their features play a melody *on the basis of and in terms of the harmonic structure I bring to bear,* those same features, however, would "sound" very different in a different "musical" setting. Ömer's telling me that what I am doing will get me into serious trouble, for example, may make him appear to me to be ignorant, invasive, and condescending, but this may well be because I have a deeply defensive character. Others who do not share my prejudice may see him as being kind to me, and even highly committed, inasmuch as he is willing to engage my anger in order to alert me to an imminent problem. The "melody" as I hear it thus reproduces the defensive "harmony" of my character, and I mistake my problematic interpretation for a simple apprehension of "fact." The problematic force of this structure is clearer if we imagine that, in this situation, Ömer is trying to warn me about the danger of my being defensive. Here, the problems in my own harmonic character will impel me to be closed to the very route to correcting those problems.

If I find my interpersonal situation unsatisfactory, then my immediate sense of how to change it will retain the same basic terms in which my existing situation is articulated. If all that is required is superficial change, then this may well be satisfactory. If there is a real problem *immanent to* the situation, however, such superficial changes will leave the basic situation untouched: they will simply provide new melodies for the same harmony. If my situation has a problem *in principle*, then it will be the harmony (and, further, the rhythm) that must change.

This can be seen clearly in the change from living as a family member to living as an independent adult (a change we do not all make successfully, as Eric Berne notes in his highly insightful book *Games People Play*). Let us consider the experience of this change with respect to the example of "home." As a child or teenager, one typically, for example, has for a home the family house, and whenever one "goes home" (from a performance, from work, after a social evening) it is to this house that one returns. Though "home" names "where *I* belong," "where I am secure," or "where I can rest," that is, though it names a functional *role* in my reality and is thus defined by who *I* am, I, as a child or teenager, experience *this house* as absolutely and objectively having the identity of home. When the child grows older and moves to a new town to attend college, a new home must be established in the new location. Here is one point where growing persons typically feel some crisis of identity, a demand for self-transformation and harmonic change. The college student often will feel divided in her sense of whether "home" is her new place in her college town or the family home. Ultimately, becoming an independent adult will require rejecting the sense of the family house as "home." That change will not be a simple "conceptual" decision: it will require *not feeling* settled in the family house and *feeling* her new location as that to which she properly returns. The same "melodic" actions—traveling from the party to this new location and traveling from the party to that old location—can take place in both harmonic settings, but what they *mean* is quite different, depending on the harmonic setting, that is, depending on which location is the real home. This shift to adopting one's adulthood is not here accomplished in or as a change of melodic action but in and as a change of harmonic context. Note too that this harmonic change is itself a change *in things*; it is the sense of "this house" that changes from "my proper place" to "not my proper place" (or vice versa).

Though the details of specific melodic narratives tend to occupy our attention and hold our interest, these melodies are not usually the site for significant change. Real personal change is change effected at the level of identity, and identity is fundamentally what is established in the rhythms and harmonies that are our platform and character rather than in the specific narratives that crown our lives. Self-transformation comes through a change in these deeper, background dimensions. It will typically require us precisely to look away from the terms of our melodic narratives and to bring the background harmonies and rhythms of our lives into explicit focus. Our identities were formed through the processes of habituation by which melodic sequences of action became transformed into harmonic backgrounds for action; self-transformation will require taking these harmonies and making them into melodies again, that is, making those harmonic dimensions of our action the specific foci of our actions.

Changing myself will mean seeing how my identity has deeply ingrained expectations for "how sense calls for further sense," that is, deeply ingrained presumptions about what goes with what, what properly follows what, and so on. Below the level of our melodic narratives, we live with the closed, cyclical narrativity of harmonic expectations; these expectations need to be discerned and challenged if we are to change. But inasmuch as these habitual patterns of harmony and rhythm are the very platform for our making sense of the world, the process of change is always working against itself, always drawing upon the very resource it is trying to change. Inasmuch as every action carries within it the harmonic and rhythmic context of my life, every action that works to change this context simultaneously does some work to reinforce it, and this makes personal change a very difficult process. Indeed, even simply reproducing my daily rhythm can make it hard for me to change the harmonic structure of my life, for I experience the harmony and rhythm in a way that is totally interwoven:

through the one, I expect the other. Though I try to end my romantic relationship with you, for example, I find that my regular morning rhythm of waking and running leads me to anticipate your company at the breakfast table when I return, and I feel driven to call you; again, the regular teenage rhythm by which my school-day afternoons unfolded—bells, class meetings, breaks, changing sunlight, growing hunger, and so on—seemed to be drawing me inexorably toward the dinner hour at home where I had to confront my abusive brother, and now the resonant rhythm of my afternoons at college brings with it a crippling sense of apprehension that inhibits my ability to interact well with my college friends at dinner, so much so that I feel I must withdraw from the company of the very people who could redefine for me what it is to be with other people. The habits of our (inter-)personality are repeated and reinforced in the rhythmic flows of our everyday temporality, and since the rhythms in which our meaningful lives are built go down to the most basic levels of the rhythms of the day and the season, we can never escape from the domain—ultimately, the simple domain of our natural embodiment—in which we will feel called back to those forms.

What our model of musical polytemporality allows us to see clearly, then, is both (1) why personal change will not be effectively carried out by our focusing at the level of our actions *as we typically articulate the terms of those actions to ourselves,* but that we must attend to the deeper levels of the temporalities of expectation that form our identity, and also (2) why such change is extremely difficult in principle, namely, because the very structures that one is working to transform are either the same as or tightly interwoven with the structures that are empowering one to engage in that process of change. The repetitive and cyclical natures of rhythm and harmony inherently work to reinforce themselves through the very actions in which we seek to change them.

This again can remind us of the incredible power and value of the erotic other. It is precisely through our dependence upon—our immersion within—the strange and autonomous power of the other that we are offered a route out of our familiar places, out of our familiar temporality, and into a new order, a new world. The other offers us a route into a different setting of the terms for our lives. The erotic other is, in many ways, both the means and the end, both the goal and the resources we draw upon, in our process of self-transformation. The erotic other is essentially interwoven in our inhabiting a new way of perceiving.

Art in Human Development

We have come upon art—creative expression—at various points throughout our study. Art is the original and originative mark, through whose inauguration an epiphany becomes available that makes possible a new way of perceiving, a new way of living, a new way of being with others. Art is the performative medium of self-transformation. Art is essentially of and essential to the human sphere, and if we look back, we can see three fundamental forms in which this self-transformative mark appears, corresponding to the three essential forms of human development. Let us begin with the child.

We have referred in general to art—creative expression—on the model of "first" or "originary" marks. For the child, there are first "first marks." Whereas our earlier discussion of marks concerned the experience of transformative marks within an already established life, the original learning of a language by the child is its original entry into an articulate, human world. In its first manifestation, in other words, the transformation-through-art is not a transformation from one world of articulate sense into a new one but is the inauguration of the world of sense as such. Like the "firstness" of bodily determinacy or of family members, this firstness of expression is one we never fully shake off: it is not an optional form *within* experience but is the very context *of* experience. For this reason, then, our relation to our "first" or "native" language is uniquely essential to our identities, and there is thus also something distinctive about the functioning of art in the establishing of this founding context. There is, in other words, a unique relationship to art that corresponds to our unique identity as "family member."

We have seen that a person is a family member, an individual, and a witness; in fact, each of these three ways of being is enacted within an artistic medium. The initial entry into the human world is accomplished through learning the language of the family—our "first language" or "mother tongue"—both in the sense of the historical, human dialect spoken and written by the family (Manitoban French, Castilian Spanish, South Boston English, Shanghai Mandarin, etc.) and in the sense of the system of gestures of recognition embodied and embedded in the things of the familiar world. What is distinctive of this art, this language, is that this language is a religious language, a language one can only relate to as "natural" or God-given inasmuch as it is trustingly taken on by the child as the true and only self-articulation of being. This is a language experienced by the child—and perhaps the whole family—as something that (1) immediately summons action, with no intermediate steps, and (2) realizes community. Our growth beyond family membership also is a growth beyond this cultic relationship to art.

This childish/religious relationship to art treats—lives out its relationship to—the mark *as* in no way optional. In fact, however, our discussion allows us to see, on the contrary, that the artistic expression is contingent and historical—a performative act of free self-origination that exceeds the worldly preconditions of its emergence—and thus is not necessitated. There is a second relationship to the artistic mark that recognizes this non-necessary character. This is our everyday stance of recognizing the artwork as a "beautiful" object of admiring contemplation, as something beyond the utilitarian terms of the everyday life.

The emergence of the individual as such is that individual's experience of growing detachment, and this adolescent withdrawal from immersion in the world is equally a withdrawal from immersion in the cultic language of the family. With emerging individuality comes the power to experience things, family members, and marks as detached objects of scrutiny, as "there," exhibiting themselves for one's private and disinterested contemplation. On the one hand, growing detachment affords one the opportunity for the dismissive trivializing that is accomplished through the objectifying gaze, which treats everything as an aesthetic surface to be judged in terms of one's personal tastes; on the other hand, it also affords one the opportunity for the apprehension of beauty.

The apprehension of beauty is the apprehension of the work as intrinsically characterized by something that *requires* one to acknowledge it: to say "I like it" is to say something about myself, but to say "It is beautiful" is to speak of a compelling character that *it* possesses. In recognizing a work as beautiful, I recognize it as having a compelling significance that I experience as something anyone should recognize. As in the childish relationship to art, in the relationship to art as beautiful, one still feels oneself impinged upon. In the childish experience, however, one *lives in* the very expression so that it is indissociably one with one's very identity, so that the presumed "necessity" of the mode of expression is not explicitly noticed but is, rather, implicitly lived. In the experience of art as beautiful, one *experiences oneself as detached from* the work, and therefore the work is not in itself necessary, but one experiences oneself as called upon to affirm explicitly the compelling character of the work. It immediately appears as having the form it should have—we experience the form of the work as "designed for" recognition by us, as if it had been waiting for our gaze to appreciate it—and this is experienced as something that should be a matter of universal recognition. This apprehension of beauty is thus of a piece with the experience of oneself as an example of universal humanity, an experience of myself as a equal instance to all others, compelled by this singular work as if by a law.

Now we have already criticized this sort of detached attitude toward the world that is presupposed in the experience of beauty inasmuch as we have criticized the presumption that the adult stance of individual, detached reflection upon an alien world is original. We have seen that this stance is not original but is a development of more basic and fundamental stances of engagement. Similarly, this detached attitude toward the artistic mark that recognizes it as "beautiful" recognizes something important *about* the artwork, but this recognition is not *adequate to* the artwork: the stance of appreciating beauty fails to recognize that this stance is itself rooted in *the meaning-opening powers of art.* The emergence of this *attitude toward* art (and the world) is itself dependent upon a changing *involvement with* creative marks, but an involvement that does not itself function according to the terms recognized by the attitude to which it gives rise. Indeed, it is *precisely* the *transformative nature* of the mark that the recognition of work as "beautiful" does not acknowledge, in large part because the detachment implied in the recognition of beauty does not allow for the recognition of the way in which the reality of the mark already impinges upon one's own reality. Though it does not *recognize* it, this detached attitude toward the mark is itself a way of *living in* an artistic transformation, is itself a stance rooted in a distinctive form of artistic engagement. Let us consider this transformation.

Though embracing a language is initially the means by which the child comes to (co-)inhabit the human world, the achieved experience of being at home in that world allows the child's relation to its language to change; indeed, establishing a home in the world allows language to change its character from "means to having a world" to "something within the world," of which the child can have an explicit experience. There is an explicit *discovery of* the power of words, of the power of gestures, into which the child develops. The child gradually comes to experience the ability of its language (in the broad sense of "language") to function outside of the realm of the family and, indeed, to build a route into a world beyond the family and a world that, in various respects, does not function according to the terms of family life. *Through* its "possession" of language, this "universal" possession, the child precisely comes to experience its free individuality, its ability to be an effective agent outside of and detached from its "homeworld" of familial immersion. The very native language possessed ("religiously") by the child affords it the power to emerge as a free individual beyond the family sphere. Within the world made available *through* the native language, possibility for play, self-expression, and artistic creativity are available to the child as ways of operating *with* that language and the meaningful world it makes available: within the world made available by language, the power of language itself comes to be something with which the child can engage. It is *by* engaging with this truly transformative dimension of the mark that the experience of detached individuality becomes a reality for the child. (This is especially seen in the powers of play therapy and art therapy to offer routes for healthy development to children dealing with complex psychological troubles rooted in unhealthy family structures.)

The art of childhood family membership is not an art of beauty but of piety, an art appearing as religion. The art of the detached individual—

or, rather, art *for* the detached individual—is an art of beauty, an art of the individual apprehension of the universal. For the child, learning the language is the same as learning the world, which means there is no distance, for the child, between language and reality—this just *is* "a house," you just *are* "mom," and so on. For the child, learning the language *is* learning to navigate reality, and things bear their names like natural properties. For the child, then, its language is the very substance of its world. In fact, though, creative expression is a work of imagination, in the sense of the ability to operate with meanings beyond the real, beyond the present, beyond the actual. In gradually coming to experience art and language *as* such, rather than simply *living in* them, the child comes to apprehend the mark *as* detached from the real, as surface rather than substance. This changed experience is what lies behind the apprehension of beauty. To apprehend art as beautiful is to apprehend it in its separation from reality, to recognize it as not "of this world." Recognizing the mark in its detachment from the real is equally recognizing that it speaks to me *as* a *detached* individual, that is, in the nonidentity of the mark with the world (which is the way it is "not just a thing" but an epiphany, as we saw earlier), the mark addresses *my* nonimmersion and thus precisely empowers my experience of the independence of my self from the familiar world of my immersion in family reality.

Through its growth in relationship to its language, then, the child undergoes an artistic revolution that results in its transformation into an adolescent individual, an individual for which an attitude *toward* art becomes possible (and typical) that makes an advance beyond the childish attitude toward art. This new attitude—the recognition of the detachment of the mark, and its attendent experience of the recognition of beauty—while enabling a liberation of the child's individuality, nonetheless fails to be adequate to the nature of art (that is, it fails to be adequate to recognizing the very artistic transformation upon which the emergence of this attitude is premised).

Like the recognition of the strange other as nonfamiliar, the recognition of beautiful art as not "of the real" invites its trivialization, either by relating to it dismissively, by treating it as simply an object of entertainment, or in general by treating it as an optional aspect of one's world. Treating art as beautiful depends on adopting this detached attitude, but this attitude is insufficient to bearing witness to the nature of the art, for as we have seen, art is not a separate, optional part of reality but is in fact the very medium in and through which our humanity is accomplished. Nonetheless, this attitude toward art as "beauty" is a kind of liberation from the pious attitude to art that one has toward one's "first language." Beauty is real, and the experience of it is integral to the accomplishing of the attitude of autonomous individuality. This detached attitude of autonomy is essential to our growth beyond the family, and, indeed, the experience of the compelling character of beauty can itself be experienced within this detached attitude as an incitation to further growth. In many ways, then, the detached experience of beauty marks an essential development in our humanity. This detached attitude is one we often carry over into adulthood as our explicit form of expectation we bring toward creative expression. Because, however, we typically do not even *notice* that we have a religious attitude to our first language, we typically vacillate between our lived, immersed religious commitment to the forms we are embedded in, and our reflective, detached attitude of admiring contemplation without noticing that these two attitudes actually conflict in principle (just as we saw earlier, we vacillate between living from the presumed givenness of our familial identity and theorizing from the presumed givenness of adult individuality).

Our humanity, however, is not complete either in our family membership or in our isolated individuality. It is ultimately realized in our responsible witnessing. Corresponding to these different possibilities for our humanity are different possibilities for our relation to art, and indeed (as we have just been seeing), these two issues of our humanity and our relation to art are integrally related. Most fundamentally, the attitude that adequately bears witness to the epiphany of art is like the contemplative attitude that recognizes creative expression as a work of imagination, but rather than being detached from this work, it recognizes in this imaginative work an imperative to which it itself cannot be indifferent. Like the pious attitude, then, this attitude recognizes in art the power of the real, but unlike the childish attitude it recognizes in the art the creative inauguration and performance of reality rather than a given natural correspondence between the expression and the substance of the real. This bearing witness—a bearing witness that is integral to our adequate witnessing to our own nature as witnesses—experiences in the artwork the imperative articulated by Rilke in his *Archaic Torso of Apollo*: "You must change your life." Bearing witness to the epiphany of the artwork is experiencing it as the imperative to self-transformation.

Though the attitude of indifferent contemplation is a power made possible through the transformation from family membership into individuality, it also is true that this attitude of relating to art in its "nonworldly" form also has lurking within it this deeper and truer relation to art that we have just described. Indeed, it is very often the case that it is precisely in the transformative, erotic times of adolescence that we are most open to this authentic witnessing to the nature of the mark. The adolescent, newly embracing the erotic realm of co-creation, is engaged in the world precisely as a site for and an imperative toward self-transformation. It is here that the authentic enthusiasm (or, indeed, deep anxiety) for the transformative vision of creative expression, for the promise of a new reality beyond the family and its values of fixed substantiality, is especially apparent. Whereas in the animal world, aging and maturing are typically the same process and the same reality, in the human world there is no guarantee that with age we come to realize more fully our human reality. On the contrary, the life of "adults" is commonly a life that has turned its back on the openness of adolescent life and has reverted to a complacent conservatism with respect to ethics, self-identity, and understanding the world and our relationship to it. In many ways, it is the enthusiasm and anxiety of adolescence—a thrilling or terrifying openness to risk upon which "adults" often turn their backs—that is the context in which our fulfillment—our maturity as persons—is possible.

Our maturity (to draw again on this imperfect concept from the biological world) comes in our witnessing to our witnessing, in our embrace of the call of our world. The call is to self-transformation that is simultaneously the deliverance of the real, honesty, and justice. This witnessing is itself enacted in and as artistic revolution. In our effort to be mature, we do not engage with art either religiously or superficially—we seek in it neither something that will substitute for our agency nor something beautiful. Art in our fullest apprehension of it is an ongoing striving to articulate the real and to enact responsibility: artists—or we, as artists—forge this path for us, and we as apprehenders of art draw on the capacity of these marks to offer us the resources for articulating our own self-transformation. Our fullest relationship to art is engaging with it *as* using the things of the world—the determinacy of the real—to bear witness to the epiphany of the real. Unlike the beautiful art of detached individuality, the art of erotic life is not held separate from ourselves and from the real but is that with which we engage precisely for the sake of joining with it in inaugurating a new reality. Unlike the art of childhood piety, however, this art that becomes our own substance is not a conservative force of self-satisfied dogmatism but is a realization of the imperative to openness. It is in this erotic artistic context that we embrace our humanity and in so doing relate to reality as such in honesty, which means relating to our humanity with a commitment to justice.

For the creative attitude, the medium of the work is experienced as a route to doing something that matters: the artist experiences the world *in* the art, in the medium, rather than experiencing the medium as *in* the world. To experience works of art as such is to experience through them this same mattering, this same enveloping of the real. The attitude of philosophy, again a witnessing to witnessing, is essentially the same. The philosopher experiences all of the determinations of the world as compelling. Her attitude to things is neither religious nor indifferent. Rather, she experiences in this the impulsion to realizing "what matters," in a way that recognizes the essentiality of her own creativity. Art and philosophy are experiences of the interconnectedness of me and it, of witness and world.

Property and Self-Transformation

We have seen the link between the experience of oneself as an autonomous individual and the emergence of a true witnessing to art as art, that is, witnessing to the creative mark as itself an epiphany and a witness to witnessing. This crucial domain of autonomous individuality is itself, as we have seen, crucially realized through the collectively sanctioned experience of private property. There is thus an important relationship between the thing-as-private-property and the thing-as-mark: property is an essential element in the realization of artistic bearing witness.

Because my social relations are such that they carve out for me a domain of free individuality, I am able to be detached from my social immersion. Private property—the way in which my community sanctions me to be free of its dictates—gives me a domain in which I am recognized to be free to revise the terms of my life, a domain in which my self-transformation is enabled. Previously we compared our detachment to the freedom of movement of the bird, or the freedom of movement we have in our ability to shift our attention. I cannot eliminate my immersion in others, but I am detached from it, in a zone of freedom of movement over which I have (sanctioned) authority. The institution of private property is our collective endorsement of your detachment, beyond your immersion in us: it gives the "I" a "place" in the real.

Private property announces the limit of the authority of (initially) the familial definition to things and (later) the social definition of things, and it defines the possibility of a meaning beyond the familiar, a meaning in which I am individually implicated. It thus defines the space of imagination, the space that legitimates the "beyond" (beyond the already established) to me and my world, and that legitimates my authority as an individual to be engaged in that beyond. We saw earlier that the inner meaning of private property is the imperative to social responsibility. We can now see as well that private property is a reality that is fundamentally defined in terms of the definitive self-transformative process of human personhood, and that it therefore has as its ultimate meaning to be a platform for this self-transformation, this human performativity. This transformative performance in turn is an artistic gesture that calls for a new community. Property enables a space for self-transformation as the birth of community.

Reality

Our own existence—our human reality—has its identity formed through the specific ways we perform ourselves. Our nature is to realize our identity through acts of creative self-expression—appropriations of our own possibilities. Our human "nature" cannot be separated logically from the historical practices through which it is realized. Because our reality is expressive, our nature is inherently historical. This historicality of our nature means that the nature of humanity, like the nature of one's own body, is a given (historical) determinacy, but one that is to be enowned, and to be enowned *as* opening toward a future.

This, our "historical" reality, furthermore, is an immersion in a world of interrelated things: indeed, it is the real determinacy of things that is the medium and embodiment of our self-expression. As the nature of our humanity develops and transforms itself historically, so too the nature of things becomes transformed. The nature of things *emerges* through the historically determinate expressive practices in which things are woven together with us.

The very nature of reality—what it is to be real—is thus itself self-transcending and emergent. It is revealed only epiphanically and accomplished only determinately and performatively. Most fundamentally, "reality" names this character of emergent, self-defining, self-transcending determinacy. Reality's "reality" needs to be realized. It is not "prefabricated," and not settled either in advance of or in alienation from the human, bodily appropriation of it. Reality is realized through our appropriation of it.

Reality thus weighs upon us, calls upon us to be its deliverance. It is experienced by us as an "ought," as a call to act. Our action—our dance—appropriates this form, responds to this call, through knowing, through speaking, through working, and through obeying. The thing is a task; it impels us to labor to set it right, to deliver it of its promise. This deliverance can take the relatively passive form of appreciation or contemplation: the path calls to be walked upon; this beautiful sunset needs to be admired; the stillness of the forest needs to be respected. This deliverance can take the form of attentive maintenance: the rosebush needs to be watered; the ensnared ferret needs to be released. This deliverance can take the familiar form of everyday habituality: the laces need to be tied; the hedge needs to be trimmed. This deliverance can take the very active form of realizing the budding needs of our human world through cultivation: the tree blocking the path needs to be moved; the land needs to be cultivated; the roof needs to be fixed. All of these forms of imperative, ranging from the call for "nonintervention" to the call for invasive action, are appeals to our active witnessing, that is, they call for us, through how we do what we do, to allow reality to be. Through our knowing, through our working, we allow the reality of the situation to shine forth, to be realized.

Most importantly, the reality that confronts us is a world of other people, and its imperatives are the imperatives of the interhuman. This reality is present in the human body lying beside me, drawing me to communicate with it bodily. My sexual advances let its reality as a locus of co-witnessing be realized. This reality is present also in the material determinations of the world, all of which bespeak their implicit immersion in the vast multiplicity of actual and possible persons into whom and toward whom these things are folded. This world calls me to moral life, to act in such a way as to acknowledge the inherent (and definitive) worth of the human face visible in all of the world's determinations. My erotic life admits and announces the other's erotic humanity. My ethical life admits and announces the humanity of reality. I can act to deny these realities, to conceal them; in so doing, I shape reality by dehumanizing it, by lying about its reality and refusing to allow its potentiality to be realized. Through erotic and ethical action, I tell the truth about the tender reality in which I am engaged, and through my actions, I allow it to be and to take up determinate shape.

We know, we work, we love; most decisively of all, we *speak*. Reality—our interhuman world—calls from us a cry, calls to us as the need to give it voice. The most fundamental way reality impinges upon us is as a reality that needs our articulation to realize it. To be real is to engage with reality and, at the most fundamental level, to be engaged *is* to express the real. Reality calls forth from us the expression through which it is brought to articulate realization. All of our action, all of our reality, is performing such an articulation in principle, and in our art and language we engage with this articulation *as* such. The imperative of the real is to announce oneself, to announce reality, to announce oneself as immersed in reality, to announce reality as immersed in oneself, and our art and language are the embrace of this imperative to articulation as such. We can ask of our actions how they enact giving a voice to the real, how they are implicitly art and language; our language is this giving voice taken up as giving voice. Reality is the imperative to such giving voice to the real.

The thing is to be known; it draws us into its inner essence, to recognize it for what it is, to set it into its truth. A situation is a puzzle until we resolve it in the insight, "*That's* what it is." This is clearest perhaps in a text, which clearly presents itself as "to be understood" and which drives us to massage it, assault it, taste it, turn it over and over, talk about it, grow irritated at it, and concentrate on it until we unite with its reality and can say, "*That's* what it means." We resolve the tensions in the things of our world and let them realize their meaningfulness through our understanding, our identifying with their inner essence. In being known, things assume their reality.

At the same time, there is ambiguity to "the real." Inasmuch as "the real" itself does not show an unequivocal face, the "correct" form for its expression is ultimately undecidable, that is, we cannot remove *our responsibility* for the judgment involved in answering to its imperative. Further, part of the call to apprehend reality truly—to "know" it—is to apprehend it *in its absoluteness*, which is to know it in its autonomy and inexhaustibility. To apprehend reality *as* the absolute is to recognize it as the source and ground of all that is. It gives itself for engagement, but that engagement releases it to reveal itself as inexhaustibly beyond. To know reality as reality, then, is to apprehend it in its self-giving and self-withholding, it is to know it as beyond knowledge. Reality as such, then, is thus both "to be known" and "to elude knowledge" or "to exceed knowledge." It is both defined by our engagement and beyond to us. This is its ultimate, constitutive ambiguity.

Reality, then, is that to which we are called to answer, but our answering will never be sufficient to it. This insufficiency, however, is not the same as failure. "Insufficiency" here means, rather, that there is nothing we can ever do that will "settle" reality or end it. The demand to realize reality is not one of many demands *within* our experience but is the inherent and thus permanent structure of experience itself.

Reality is, then, that which calls forth ethical action. It is what calls us to be humans, to be witnesses to the real. Metaphysics thus cannot be divorced from epistemology and ethics. Knowledge, similarly, is knowing reality *as* the call to duty, understanding the ambiguity that is the essence of the thing. Epistemology thus cannot be divorced from metaphysics and ethics. Finally, we cannot act ethically except insofar as we express the truth about the other, recognize the other's reality. Ethics thus cannot be divorced from epistemology and metaphysics. This does not mean, however, that these separate domains necessarily "accompany" each other; rather, they are different perspectives on *the same domain*.

Reality is ethics *throughout*: determinacy *is* the call to the honest deliverance of its reality. Reality is the need to understand *throughout*: the draw to realize our immersion through the insightful identification with the essence of things that supersedes our alienation and detachment and lets us embody ourselves in them and live through them. Reality is language *throughout*: the site of the articulation and communication of the bodily, epiphanic—human—world. Reality is thus the call to philosophy *throughout*: it is the call to do metaphysics, to tell the truth about the nature of reality, through the expression of insight by which we build a communicative co-witnessing with others.

Honesty

Property, language, metaphysics, erotics—these are all ways of conceiving the reality that is creative interpersonal recognition, the performative accomplishment of co-witnessing. All of these, in other words, ultimately answer to the demands of our being with others. Reality is inherently characterized by our being with others, and all of our forms of engagement have an immanent dynamism whereby this fact about their essential nature will ultimately come to the surface. Through our engagements, we are dealing with others, and the demands of ethical life are thus ever-present.

Our dealing with others is an engagement with the imperative to do justice to the reality of co-witnessing, to be true to the bonds that constitute our humanity. The imperative that resounds *throughout* our engagement with reality is "tell the truth." We are called to recognize adequately, in a recognition that itself entails expression. We must know and act the truth, learn and express the interwoven nature of others and things, the nature of reality as the realm for humanity and justice. The imperative to honesty is ultimately the imperative to express ourselves, through word and deed, in such a way as to recognize the ambiguity of reality and the pervasiveness of humanity, the pervasiveness of the ethical. This is ultimately no different than the imperative to perceive things well.

The thing is a metaphysical magnet, singular and universal, independent from us and reliant on our knowing of it, a multifaceted ambiguity that affords a multiplicity of possible grasps and that shows itself differently in coordination with different modes of approaching it. Just as perceptually the thing's front side intimates its back side, and in general every perceptual aspect points to the further possible perceptual aspects on its horizon, so too does each facet of the thing's ambiguity have the other facets lurking within it. The nature of the thing is that it does not give itself to perception all at once but presents itself as a site for progressive explication, and this explication can run down avenues of different types: in a tighter intertwining of our own bodily powers with the thing's focal specificity, we can more thoroughly examine the immediately perceptible aspects of the thing's particularity by attending to its coloration, examining its other sides, and in general isolating through our bodily actions moments of its total face in acts of perceptual explication; we can investigate its modes of interaction with other things in a process of "scientific" investigation that seeks to understand universal principles that are at play in the world of things taken as an indifferent, detached surface; we can seek through the thing the humanity that articulates itself therein, inasmuch as we recognize a gesture being expressed through the makeup of a situation; we can draw from the thing an insight into the nature of reality as such in philosophical investigations of the sort undertaken here. Down a multiplicity of avenues (each of which occludes the others), the possibility of "seeing better" is always offered to us by perception. We can always "see better," and this development always involves an intensification of our own involvement, an effort of creativity through which we develop our own reality as much as we discern what was lying in wait. Telling the truth means answering to this demand for further explication through creative expression and self-development.

As the site of the articulation of the bonds that constitute humanity, the world of perception demands this honesty in a specially charged fashion. The recognition demanded is the recognition of the opening of others onto the realm of creative humanity. That is, we are called to recognize in things the possibility they offer for others to realize their humanity. Equally the creative expression demanded of us is the realizing of our own most essential possibilities, our humanity. The ultimate demand for explication—for "seeing better"—that perception places upon us is the demand to be true to ourselves in and as being true to others, to affirm a human co-witnessing by enacting it.

In our actions—our own perceptible self-determination or self-articulation—we are fundamentally answering to this demand of co-witnessing. Our actions are *essentially* human actions, whether we so intend them or not, and it is in relation to this imperative to honesty as co-witnessing that we can assess the ultimate import of our behavior— our *human* behavior. In all of our actions we engage the humanity of others, singly and as a whole. Through our expressions we can break another person: we can grab hold of her or his tender essence and bruise or destroy it. Through our words we can allow another to be: we can nurture that tender essence through expressions that pay adequate respect to the freedom and creativity that is the core of the other's determinacy. We can dehumanize our world and impede the flowering of human reality as a whole through actions that deny the ambiguity of things and (thereby) the inherently ethical demands placed upon us by all such things, or we can, through our actions, work to acknowledge and respect global humanity through our local dealings with all determinations of reality. And through all of this our own personal humanity is at stake: our own humanity as witness to epiphany is what is denied or affirmed, suppressed or realized, through these actions. Our freedom is the demand that we realize our freedom, that we assume the responsibility for engendering justice in the creative engendering of a human environment in which we assume our own responsible personhood through recognizing and nurturing the responsible personhood of others and through recognizing and nurturing this principle as such.

Justice

Reality is the epiphany of the imperative to tell the truth. The reception of this imperative is not simple. This is the imperative to be true to our humanity, to enact a co-witnessing, but our humanity, our co-witnessing, is of an inherently ambiguous nature. Telling the truth is not a matter of uttering grammatically sound sentences that "correspond correctly" to states of affairs: it is a matter of wisdom, a matter of creatively taking responsibility for caring for the ambiguous, tender essence of this world. How we are true to ourselves and how we respect the humanity of others is not a matter of "corresponding correctly" to some existent state of affairs but is a creative expression of how the truth of the multiplicity of possible aspects of people's determinacy is to be realized. Our recognition will answer to what lies in wait, but it will also be a decision, and it will be a selective evaluation within a field of possibilities, some of which will be refused or excluded.

The ambiguity of our nature is our immersion-detachment, and this ambiguity sets the parameters for honesty. (1) Because we are inherently immersed in things and in other people, our own nature always offers up a multiplicity of determinations as possible centers of our reality. We *are* family members. We *are* black women. We *are* home owners. We *are* prairie dwellers. We *are* right-handed. We *are* candy lovers. Our humanity cannot be respected except through the determinacies in which we are immersed. These determinacies, however, are multiple and conflicting, and our endorsement of humanity—our own or that of another— will require a selection of which of these determinations are the essential ones. (2) Because we are inherently detached from things and from other people, we *are not* any of the determinate identities in which we are immersed, and we must not be confused with them. Honest respect for these determinacies must be such as to acknowledge the way they underdetermine our nature. It is, then, only through a commitment to our determinacies that we can be honest, but we are honest only if we are committed to them as insufficient grounds on their own for determining how we are to act. This two-sided imperative has two implications.

The ambiguous demands of our nature entail, first, that determinacies cannot be abstracted from their lived context in human life in order to establish a rule for behavior: it is not that case that "a father" or "a lover" or "a black woman" or "a Catholic" must act a certain way, without reference to the immersed-detached life of the one who is "father" or "lover," and so on. On the contrary, these are the identities one inhabits, and it is precisely the moral demand of one's character as witness that one *not* be able to be *determined* by them and to absolve oneself of the responsibility of judgment: these identities, by their very nature, call to us to be wise in *determining* how to realize them responsibly. The first implication, then, of our ambiguous nature is that we are unavoidably called to wisdom. The ambiguous demands of our nature entail, second, that an honest recognition of one's humanity—our own or that of another—will require a privileging of the self-transformative, creative core of one's relation to one's determinateness. The meaning of our lives and the demands of responsible living are not matters that have already been settled: they are precisely matters that call for us to go beyond the past and to realize the possibilities of fulfillment creatively. The call to wisdom cannot be separated from the call to openness.

Honesty requires recognizing that I am a family member; it requires recognizing that I am not just a family member. It requires recognizing the multiplicity of engagements *by which* I am something determinate but also recognizing that the *human* character of that determinateness is its propulsion toward free co-witnessing. There is an honesty in honoring and respecting family ties, as there is a dishonesty in failing to recognize our essential rootedness in them. There is an honesty in recognizing an allegiance to our "professional" involvements, to being a "company man," as there is a dishonesty in denying our reliance upon such participation. And yet there is a fundamental dishonesty in insisting upon the family as *the* context of human reality and a dishonesty in treating the business market as *the* proper realm of duty. These determinacies are one-sided, and both the family and the marketplace are bonds—institutions—of human life that are inherently premised on a dishonest closedness toward essential aspects of our humanity: familial loyalty denies our essentially self-transcending character, and the economic marketplace denies our immersion, our nondiscrete, nondetached, nonindifferent determinacy. There is an honesty in recognizing—through our practices—an essentiality to these facets of our humanity, but a fundamental dishonesty in attributing to them primacy for defining our human reality. An analogous point can be made with respect to our "patriotic" attachment to our law, language, history, and culture. There is an honesty in recognizing that I am a citizen of a particular culture, as there is a dishonesty in disavowing such embeddedness (as Socrates makes clear in Plato's *Crito*), but equally there is a dishonesty in thinking that my culture is *the* source of meaning (as Socrates makes clear in Plato's *Apology*). The issue, again, is whether these institutions of our patriotism and cultural membership are embraced in a way that is true to our immersed-detached character, which is especially an issue of our immersion-detachment with respect to others, that is, an issue of co-witnessing.

It is our erotic character that is the precise locus of our ambiguous essence as immersed-detached creators of human co-witnessing. Erotic life is just the engagement with this ambiguity of our nature and with the realm of tender meaningfulness that it opens up to us as the sphere of self-determining human communication. It is the sphere in which we share with others in and as the very process of creative, mutual individualization. The erotic sphere is the sphere of emerging into free individuality precisely as the imperative to "keep one's word," to be consistent in one's creative expression and articulation of the shared world of human life. It is as such an individual—a *person*—and not as, specifically, a family member or a company man, a church member or a party representative, an Iranian or an African American, or a Canadian or a Jew that one most truly belongs to the realm of honesty. The demand to tell the truth—though inherently complex, conflicted, and ambiguous—ultimately reveals itself as the imperative to be such a person and to realize others as such. This is the essential character of justice. Justice means being a person by facilitating the realization of the personhood (the personality) of others.

The imperatives of ethics, then, look initially to be very close to the imperatives of psychological development and emotional maturity. Being human means growing into one's personhood through the demands of family life, the struggles of adolescence, and the responsibilities of adult life. It means developing the bodily capacities for perceptual recognition, the powers of concentration, attention, and memory necessary for systematic interpretation and understanding, the self-interpretive and self-critical habits necessary for emotional self-control, the facility with art and language necessary to engage with others in erotic practices of engagement and sharing. Ethics, first and foremost, announces this need to *grow up*, to develop the ability to handle one's bodily, emotional, social, and interpersonal world, to keep one's word, to mature *into* a free participant in human co-witnessing.

We can see further into this imperative and recognize that ethics itself matures into the imperative to care for others. It is the imperative to nurture children, to provide and participate in the education of the new generation, which equally requires a care for the past: this is witnessing to witnessing as the teaching that is the passing on of our reality, the maintenance of the tradition of witnessing, not as dead repetition but as creative transformation. It is the imperative to seek and to provide therapy in our struggles with the complex tensions of our interpersonal lives. It is the imperative to enter into communities of law and to recognize ourselves as responsible agents of the law.

Beyond all of this, it is the imperative to communicate with others through all possible avenues in a project of realizing through creative articulation a shared humanity, a co-witnessing to the epiphany of reality. This witnessing to reality can only be effected within a fundamental openness: an openness to the "wonders" of things, and an openness to the self-transformative change for which witnessing to their nature calls. It is this final articulation that I understand as the definition of the practice of philosophy. Ultimately, the imperative definitive of things—the imperative to justice, to humanity, to personhood—is the imperative to philosophy. Philosophy is bearing witness to epiphany.

BIBLIOGRAPHY

♦♦♦

Albee, Edward. *Who's Afraid of Virginia Woolf?* New York: Signet, 1983.

Anderson, Douglas. *Philosophy Americana: Making Philosophy at Home in American Culture.* New York: Fordham University Press, 2006.

Aristotle. *The Complete Works of Aristotle.* 2 vols. Edited by Jonathan Barnes. Princeton, NJ: Princeton University Press, 1984.

Bachelard, Gaston. *The Poetics of Space.* Boston: Beacon Press, 1994.

Bateson, Gregory. *Steps to an Ecology of Mind.* Chicago: University of Chicago Press, 2000.

Beckman-Long, Brenda. "The Narratee as Confessor in Margaret Laurence's *The Fire-Dwellers.*" *Literature and Theology* 17:2 (2003): 113–26.

Bell, Silvia M. "The Development of the Concept of Other as Related to Infant-Mother Attachment." *Child Development* 41:2 (1970): 291–311.

Bergson, Henri. *Matter and Memory.* Translated by Nancy Margaret Paul and W. Scott Palmer. New York: Humanities Press, 1978.

Berne, Eric. *Games People Play.* New York: Grove, 1964.

Blum, Lawrence A. *Moral Perception and Particularism.* Cambridge: Cambridge University Press, 1994.

Böll, Heinrich. *The Clown.* Translated by Leila Vennewitz. New York: Avon Books, 1975.

Bollas, Christopher. *The Mystery of Things.* New York: Routledge, 1999.

Borgo, David. *Sync or Swarm: Improvising Music in a Complex Age.* New York: Continuum, 2005.

Bredlau, Susan. "Learning to See: Merleau-Ponty and the Navigation of Terrains." *Chiasmi International* 8 (2006): 191–200.

Brudner, Alan. *The Unity of the Common Law: Studies in Hegelian Jurisprudence.* Berkeley: University of California Press, 1995.

Bullowa, M., ed. *Before Speech: The Beginnings of Human Communication.* Cambridge: Cambridge University Press, 1979.

Burkert, Walter. *Greek Religion.* Translated by John Raffan. Cambridge, MA: Harvard University Press, 2006.

Caplan, Jane, and John Torpey, eds. *Documenting Individual Identity: The Development of State Practices in the Modern World.* Princeton, NJ: Princeton University Press, 2001.

Casey, Edward S. *Getting Back into Place: Toward a Renewed Understanding of the Place-World.* Bloomington: Indiana University Press, 1993.

Christman, John, ed. *The Inner Citadel: Essays on Individual Autonomy.* Oxford: Oxford University Press, 1989.

———. "The Search for Agency: Comments on John Russon's *Human Experience.*" *Dialogue* 45 (2006): 327–36.

Ciavatta, David. "Hegel on Owning One's Own Body." *Southern Journal of Philosophy* 43:1 (2005): 1–24.

———. "The Unreflective Bonds of Intimacy: Hegel on Family Ties and the Modern Person." *Philosophical Forum* 37:2 (2006): 153–81.

Cobb, Edith. *The Ecology of Imagination in Children.* Dallas, TX: Spring Publications, 1993.

Collingwood, R. G. *The Principles of Art.* Oxford: Clarendon Press, 1938.

———. *Speculum Mentis.* Oxford: Clarendon Press, 1924.

Davidson, Joyce. *Phobic Geographies: The Phenomenology and Spatiality of Identity.* Aldershot and Burlington, VT: Ashgate, 2003.

de Beauvoir, Simone, *The Ethics of Ambiguity.* Translated by Bernard Frechtman. New York: Citadel Press, 1991.

Deleuze, Gilles, and Félix Guattari. *L'Anti-Oedipe.* Paris: Éditions de Minuit, 1972. Translated by Robert Hurley, Mark Seem, and Helen R. Lane as *Anti-Oedipus: Capitalism and Schizophrenia.* New York: Viking, 1977.

Derrida, Jacques. *Acts of Religion.* Edited by Gil Anidjar. New York: Routledge, 2002.

———. *Apories*. Paris: Éditions Galilée, 1996. Translated by Thomas Dutoit as *Aporias*. Stanford, CA: Stanford University Press, 1993.

———. *La Voix et la Phénomène*. Paris: Presses Universitaires de France, 1972. Translated by David B. Allison as *Speech and Phenomena, and Other Essays on Husserl's Theory of Signs*. Evanston, IL: Northwestern University Press, 1973.

———. *Le Toucher, Jean-Luc Nancy*. Paris, Éditions Galilée, 2000. Translated by Christine Irizarry as *On Touching—Jean-Luc Nancy*. Stanford, CA: Stanford University Press, 2005.

———. *Memoirs of the Blind: The Self-Portrait and Other Ruins*. Translated by Pascale-Anne Brault and Michael Naas. Chicago: University of Chicago Press, 1993.

———. *Of Hospitality*. Translated by Rachel Bowlby. Stanford, CA: Stanford University Press, 2000.

———. *On Cosmopolitanism and Forgiveness*. Translated by Mark Dooley and Michael Hughes. London and New York: Routledge, 2001.

Dewey, John. *Human Nature and Conduct*. New York: The Modern Library, 1957.

———. *Individualism Old and New*. Amherst, NY: Prometheus Books, 1999.

Dickens, Charles. *Barnaby Rudge*. Oxford: Oxford University Press, 1987.

Dillard, Annie. *Pilgrim at Tinker Creek*. New York: Harper Perenniel, 2007.

Dyl, Jennifer, and Seymour Wapner. "Age and Gender Differences in the Nature, Meaning and Function of Cherished Possessions for Children and Adolescents." *Journal of Experimental Child Psychology* 62 (1996): 340–77.

Eisenberg-Berg, Nancy, Robert Haake, Michael Hand, and Edward Sadalia. "Effects of Instructions Concerning Ownership of a Toy on Preschoolers' Sharing and Defensive Behaviors." *Developmental Psychology* 15:4 (1979): 460–61.

Emerson, Ralph Waldo. *Representative Men*. Boston, MA: Adamant Media, 2000.

———. *Nature and Selected Essays*. Harmondsworth: Penguin, 2003.

Fasig, Lauren G. "Toddlers' Understanding of Ownership: Implications for Self-Concept Development." *Social Development* 9:3 (2000): 370–82.

Faulkner, William. *The Old Man.* New York: Signet Books, 1948.

———. *The Sound and The Fury* (corrected text). New York: Vintage International, 1990.

Feldman, Karen. *Binding Words: Conscience and Rhetoric in Hobbes, Hegel, and Heidegger.* Evanston, IL: Northwestern University Press, 2006.

Fichte, Johann Gottlieb. *Grundlage der gesammten Wissenschaftslehre.* In *Fichtes Werke, Band 1, zur theoretischen Philosophie I.* Hrsg. v. I. H. Fichte. Berlin: Walter de Gruyter and Co., 1971. Translated by Peter Heath and John Lachs as *The Science of Knowledge.* Cambridge: Cambridge University Press, 1982.

Fillion, Réal. *Multicultural Dynamics and the Ends of History: Exploring Kant, Hegel, and Marx.* Ottawa: University of Ottawa Press, 2008.

Fogel, Alan. "A Relational Perspective on the Development of Self and Emotion." Chapter 5 of *Identity and Emotion: Development through Self-Organization.* Edited by Harke A. Bosma and E. Saskiakurnen. Cambridge: Cambridge University Press, 2005.

Frances, Allen, and Peter Dunn. "The Attachment-Autonomy Conflict in Agoraphobia." *International Journal of Psycho-Analysis* 56:4 (1975): 435–39.

Freud, Sigmund. *Civilization and Its Discontents.* Translated by James Strachey. New York: Norton, 1961.

Furby, L. "Possessions: Toward a Theory of Their Meaning and Function throughout the Life Cycle." In *Lifespan Development and Behavior,* vol. 1, ed. P. B. Baltes, 297–336. New York: Academy Press, 1978.

Gadamer, Hans-Georg. *Philosophical Hermeneutics.* Berkeley: University of California Press, 1992.

———. *Truth and Method.* London: Continuum, 2004.

Gallagher, Shaun. *How the Body Shapes the Mind.* Oxford: Oxford University Press, 2005.

Gibson, James J. *The Ecological Approach to Visual Perception.* Hillsdale, NJ: Erlbaum, 1986.

Gilligan, Carol. *In a Different Voice.* Cambridge MA: Harvard University Press, 1982.

———. "Moral Orientation and Moral Development." In *Ethics,* ed. James Sterba, 552–63. Oxford: Oxford University Press, 2000.

Goethe, Johann Wolfgang. *Theory of Colours.* Cambridge: MIT Press, 1970.

Goldstein, Alan J., and Dianne L. Chambless. "A Reanalysis of Agoraphobia." *Behaviour Therapy* 9 (1978): 47–59.

Gopnik, Alison, Andrew N. Meltzoff, and Patricia K. Kuhl. *The Scientist in the Crib: Minds, Brains, and How Children Learn.* New York: Morrow, 1999.

Hay, Dale F. "Cooperative Interactions and Sharing between Very Young Children and Their Parents." *Developmental Psychology* 15:6 (1979): 647–53.

———. "Yours and Mine: Toddlers Talk about Possessions with Familiar Peers." *British Journal of Developmental Psychology* 24:1 (2006): 39–52.

Hegel, G. W. F. *Elements of the Philosophy of Right.* Translated by H. B. Nisbet. Cambridge: Cambridge University Press, 1991.

———. *Phänomenologie des Geistes.* Hrsg. v. Hans-Friedrich Wessels und Heinrich Clairmont. Hamburg: Felix Meiner, 1988. Translated by A. V. Miller as *Phenomenology of Spirit.* Oxford: Oxford University Press, 1977.

Heidegger, Martin. *Basic Concepts.* Translated by Gary E. Aylesworth. Bloomington: Indiana University Press, 1993.

———. *Basic Writings.* 2d ed. Edited by David Farrell Krell. New York: Harper, 1992.

———. *Beiträge zur Philosophie (vom Ereignis).* Gesamtausgabe Bd. 65. Frankfurt: Klostermann, 1989. Translated by Parvis Emad and Kenneth Maly as *Contributions to Philosophy (From Enowning).* Bloomington: Indiana University Press, 1999.

———. *Hölderlin's Hymn "The Ister."* Translated by William MacNeill and Julia Davis. Bloomington: Indiana University Press, 1996.

———. *Sein und Zeit,* 5. Auflage. Tübingen: Max Niemeyer, 1941. Translated by Joan Stambaugh as *Being and Time.* Albany: State University of New York Press, 1996.

———. *Was Heisst Denken?* Tübingen: Max Niemeyer, 1971. Translated by J. Glenn Gray as *What Is Called Thinking?* New York: Harper Perenniel, 1976.

Hoff, Shannon. "Law, Right, and Forgiveness: The Remains of Antigone in the *Phenomenology of Spirit.*" *Philosophy Today* 50, SPEP Supplement (2006): 31–38.

―――. "Restoring Antigone to Ethical Life: Nature and Sexual Difference in Hegel's *Phenomenology of Spirit.*" *Owl of Minerva* 38 (2007): 77–99.

Hölderlin, Friedrich. *Odes and Epigrams*, in *Poems and Fragments.* Translated by Michael Hamburger. London: Anvil Press Poetry, 2004.

Homer. *Odyssey.* Translated by Richmond Lattimore. New York: Harper Perenniel, 1999.

Houlgate, Stephen. *The Opening of Hegel's Logic.* West Lafayette, IN: Purdue University Press, 2006.

Husserl, Edmund. *Cartesianische Meditationen.* Hamburg: Felix Meiner, 1987. Translated by Dorion Cairns as *Cartesian Meditations.* The Hague: Martinus Nijhoff, 1960.

Jacobson, Kirsten. "Agoraphobia and Hypochondria as Disorders of Dwelling." *International Studies in Philosophy* 36:2 (2004): 31–44.

―――. "The Interpersonal Expression of Human Spatiality: A Phenomenological Interpretation of *Anorexia Nervosa.*" *Chiasmi International* 8 (2006): 157–74.

Kant, Immanuel. *Critique of Judgment.* Translated by Werner S. Pluhar. Indianapolis: Hackett, 1987.

―――. *Critique of Pure Reason.* Translated by Norman Kemp Smith. New York: St. Martin's Press, 1929.

―――. *The Doctrine of Virtue. Part II of The Metaphysics of Morals.* Translated by Mary Gregor. Philadelphia: University of Pennsylvania Press, 1964.

―――. *On Education.* Translated by Annette Churton. Mineola, NY: Dover Publications, 2003.

Karen, Robert. *Becoming Attached: First Relationships and How They Shape Our Capacity to Love.* Oxford: Oxford University Press, 1998.

Kohlberg, Lawrence. *The Philosophy of Moral Development.* San Francisco: Harper and Row, 1981.

Kristeva, Julia. *Revolution in Poetic Language.* Translated by Margaret Waller. New York: Columbia University Press, 1984.

Laing, R. D. *The Divided Self.* London: Penguin, 1990.

―――. *The Politics of the Family.* Toronto: Canadian Broadcasting Company, 1969.

Lakoff, George, and Rafael E. Núñez. *Where Mathematics Comes From: How the Embodied Mind Brings Mathematics into Being.* New York: Basic Books, 2000.

Laurence, Margaret. *The Fire-Dwellers.* Chicago: University of Chicago Press, 1993.

Lawlor, Leonard. *Derrida and Husserl: The Basic Problem of Phenomenology.* Bloomington: Indiana University Press, 2002.

———. Review of John Russon, *Human Experience. Continental Philosophy Review* 39 (2006): 215–22.

Levine, Mark. *The Jazz Theory Book.* Petaluma, CA: Sher Music Co., 1995.

Locke, John. *Two Treatises of Government.* Cambridge: Cambridge University Press, 1988.

Lysaker, John. *You Must Change Your Life: Poetry, Philosophy, and the Birth of Sense.* University Park: Pennsylvania State University Press, 2002.

Machan, Tibor R., ed. *The Main Debate: Communism versus Capitalism.* New York: Random House, 1987.

Maclaren, Kym. "Emotional Disorder and the *Mind-Body Problem*: A Case Study of Alexithymia." *Chiasmi International* 8 (2006): 139–55.

———. "Intercorporeity, Intersubjectivity and the Problem of 'Letting Others Be.'" *Chiasmi International* 4 (2002): 187–210.

———. "Life Is Inherently Expressive: A Merleau-Pontian Response to Darwin's *The Expression of Emotions in Men and Animals.*" *Chiasmi International* 7 (2005): 241–61.

Marcus, Clare Cooper. *House as a Mirror of Self: Exploring the Deeper Meaning of Home.* San Francisco: Conari Press, 1997.

Marratto, Scott. "Russon's Pharmacy: Mental Illness and the Therapy of Philosophy in *Human Experience.*" Forthcoming.

Marx, Karl. "Critique of Hegel's Philosophy of Right." In *Early Writings*, trans. Rodney Livingstone and Gregor Benton. London: Pelican, 1992.

Marx, Karl, and Friedrich Engels. *Selected Works.* 3 vols. Moscow: Progress Publishers, 1969.

McCumber, John. *Reshaping Reason: Toward a New Philosophy.* Bloomington: Indiana University Press, 2004.

Melville, Herman. *Moby Dick: Or, The Whale.* New York: Modern Library, 2000.

Merleau-Ponty, Maurice. *Consciousness and the Acquisition of Language.* Translated by Hugh J. Silverman. Evanston, IL: Northwestern University Press, 1973.

———. *La Phénoménologie de la Perception.* Paris: Éditions Gallimard, 1945. Translated into English by Colin Smith as *Phenomenology of Perception.* London: Routledge and Kegan Paul, 1962.

Minuchin, Salvador, and H. Charles Fishman. *Family Therapy Techniques.* Cambridge, MA: Harvard University Press, 1981.

Morris, David. "Ecstatic Body, Ecstatic Nature: Perception as Breaking with the World." *Chiasmi International* 8 (2006): 201–17.

———. "The Open Figure of Experience and Mind." *Dialogue* 45 (2006): 315–26.

———. *The Sense of Space.* Albany: State University of New York Press, 2004.

Murdoch, Iris. *The Sovereignty of Good.* London: Routledge and Kegan Paul, 1970.

Nagel, Thomas. "Sexual Perversion." *Journal of Philosophy* 66:1 (1969): 5–17.

Nietzsche, Friedrich. *Beyond Good and Evil.* Translated by R. J. Hollingdale. Harmondsworth: Penguin, 2003.

———. *The Birth of Tragedy and Other Writings.* Edited by Raymond Geuss and Ronald Speirs. Cambridge: Cambridge University Press, 1999.

———. *On the Genealogy of Morals: A Polemic.* Translated by Douglas Smith. Oxford: Oxford University Press, 1998.

Noddings, Nel. *Caring: A Feminine Approach to Ethics and Moral Education.* Berkeley: University of California Press, 1984.

Noë, Alva. *Action in Perception.* Cambridge, MA: MIT Press, 2004.

O'Connor, Kevin J. *The Play Therapy Primer.* 2d ed. New York: Wiley, 2000.

Ottman, Robert W. *Elementary Harmony: Theory and Practice.* Englewood Cliffs, NJ: Prentice Hall, 1961.

Paterson, Isabel. *The God of the Machine.* New Brunswick, NJ: Transaction Publishers, 1993),

Pipp-Siegel, Sandra, and Carol Foltz. "Toddlers' Acquisition of Self/Other Knowledge: Ecological and Interpersonal Aspects of Self and Other." *Child Development* 68:1 (1997): 69–79.

Plato. *Complete Works*. Edited by John M. Cooper. Indianapolis, IN: Hackett, 1997.

Rich, Adrienne. "Compulsory Heterosexuality and Lesbian Existence." In *Blood, Bread, and Poetry: Selected Prose, 1979–1985*, 23–75. New York: Norton, 1994.

Rilke, Rainer Maria. *The Selected Poetry of Rainer Maria Rilke*. Translated by Stephen Mitchell. New York: Vintage, 1989.

Rochat, P., ed. *The Self in Early Infancy*. New York: North-Holland-Elsevier Science Publishers, 1995.

Rose, Carol. "The Comedy of the Commons: Custom, Commerce, and Inherently Public Property." *University of Chicago Law Review* 53:3 (Summer 1986): 711–81.

Ross, Sinclair. *As For Me and My House*. Lincoln: University of Nebraska Press, 1978.

Russon, John. "Eros and Education: Plato's Transformative Epistemology." *Laval Théologique et Philosophique* 56 (2000): 113–25.

———. "Hegel, Heidegger, and Ethnicity: The Ritual Basis of Self-Identity." *Southern Journal of Philosophy* 33 (1995): 509–32.

———. *Human Experience: Philosophy, Neurosis, and the Elements of Everyday Life*. Albany: State University of New York Press, 2003.

———. "Merleau-Ponty and the New Science of the Soul." *Chiasmi International* 8 (2006): 129–38.

———. "Spatiality and Self-Consciousness: Originary Passivity in Kant, Merleau-Ponty, and Derrida." *Chiasmi International* 9 (2007): 219–32.

———. "Temporality and the Future of Philosophy in Hegel." *International Philosophical Quarterly* 48 (2008): 59–68.

———. "The Bodily Unconscious in Freud's *Three Essays*." In *Rereading Freud: Psychoanalysis through Philosophy*, ed. Jon Mills, 33–50. Albany: State University of New York Press, 2004.

———. "The Elements of Everyday Life: Three Lessons from Ancient Greece." *Philosophy in the Contemporary World* 13:2 (2006): 84–90.

———. "The Intersubjective Path from Body to Mind." *Dialogue* 45 (2006): 307–14.

———. "The Virtue of Stoicism: On First Principles in Philosophy and Life." *Dialogue* 45 (2006): 347–54.

Sacks, Oliver. *An Anthropologist on Mars: Seven Paradoxical Tales.* New York: Vintage, 1996.

———. *The Man Who Mistook His Wife for a Hat and Other Clinical Tales.* New York: Touchstone, 1998.

———. "When Music Heals." *Parade Magazine* (March 31, 2002): 4–5.

Sartre, Jean-Paul. *L'Être et le Néant: Essai d'ontologie phénoménologique.* Paris: Gallimard, 1943. Translated by Hazel E. Barnes as *Being and Nothingness.* New York: Philosophical Library, 1956.

Schiller, Friedrich. *On the Aesthetic Education of Man.* Translated by Elizabeth M. Wilkinson and L. A. Willoughby. Oxford: Clarendon Press, 1967.

Schmidtz, David. "The Institution of Property." *Social Philosophy and Policy* 11 (1994): 42–62.

Schönberg, Arnold. *Structural Functions of Harmony.* New York: Norton, 1969.

———. *Theory of Harmony.* Translated by Roy E. Carter. London: Faber and Faber, 1978.

Schwenger, Peter. *The Tears of Things: Melancholy and Physical Objects.* Minneapolis: University of Minnesota Press, 2006.

Sepper, Dennis L. "Goethe and the Poetics of Science." *Janushead* 8:1 (2005): 207–27.

Sheets-Johnstone, Maxine. "Phenomenology and Agency: Methodological and Theoretical Issues in Strawson's 'The Self.'" *Journal of Consciousness Studies* 6:4 (1999): 48–69.

Sophocles. *Antigone.* Translated by Richmond Lattimore. In *Greek Tragedies,* vol. 1, 2d ed., ed. David Grene and Richmond Lattimore, 177–232. Chicago: University of Chicago Press, 1991.

Sparshott, Francis. *Taking Life Serious: A Study of the Argument of the Nicomachean Ethics.* Toronto: University of Toronto Press, 1996.

Stern, Daniel N. *The Interpersonal World of the Infant: A View from Psychoanalysis and Developmental Psychology.* New York: Basic Books, 1985.

Stravinsky, Igor. *Poetics of Music in the Form of Six Lessons.* Cambridge, MA: Harvard University Press, 1993.

Stuhr, John J. *Genealogical Pragmatism: Philosophy, Experience, and Community.* Albany: State University of New York Press, 1997.

————. "Some Experiences, Some Values, and Some Philosophies: On Russon's Account of Experience, Neurosis, and Philosophy." *Dialogue* 45 (2006): 337–45.

Talero, Maria. "Intersubjectivity and Intermodal Perception." *Chiasmi International* 8 (2006): 175–89.

————. "Merleau-Ponty and the Bodily Subject of Learning." *International Philosophical Quarterly* 46 (2006): 191–204.

————. "Perception, Normativity, and Selfhood in Merleau-Ponty: The Spatial 'Level' and Existential Space." *Southern Journal of Philosophy* 43 (2005): 443–61.

————. "Temporality and the Therapeutic Subject: The Phenomenology of Transference, Remembering, and Working-Through." In *Rereading Freud: Psychoanalysis Through Philosophy*, ed. Jon Mills, 165–80. Albany: State University of New York Press, 2004.

Thucydides. *History of the Peloponnesian War.* Translated by Rex Warner. Harmondsworth: Penguin, 1972.

Varela, Francisco. *Ethical Know-How: Action, Wisdom, and Cognition.* Stanford, CA: Stanford University Press, 1999.

Veblen, Thorsten. "The Beginning of Ownership." *American Journal of Sociology* 4 (1898–1899): 352–65.

Whitman, Walt. "I Sing the Body Electric." In *Walt Whitman: The Complete Poems*, ed. Francis Murphy, 127–35. Harmondsworth: Penguin, 2005.

Winnicott, D. W. *The Child, the Family, and the Outside World.* Harmondsworth: Penguin, 1968.

————. *Home Is Where We Start From: Essays by a Psychoanalyst.* New York: Norton, 1986.

Woolf, Virginia. *The Waves.* Oxford: Oxford University Press, 1998.

Wordsworth, William. "My Heart Leaps Up When I Behold." In *William Wordsworth: The Major Works*, ed. Stephen Gill, 246. Oxford: Oxford University Press, 2000.

Wright, John R. "Transcendence without Reality." *Philosophy* 80 (2005): 361–84.

X, Malcolm. *Malcolm X Speaks.* New York: Grove/Atlantic, 1994.

INDEX

♦♦♦

149